It's My Life!

A Power Journal for Teens

A Workout for Your Mind

Tian Dayton, Ph.D.

Health Communications, Inc.
Deerfield Beach, Florida

www.hci-online.com

Publisher: Health Communications, Inc.
            3201 S.W. 15th Street
            Deerfield Beach, FL 33442-8190

Cover and inside book design by Lawna Patterson Oldfield

To
Marina and Alex,
two of my
greatest teachers.

Contents

My Photograph ▪ Collages ▪ Introducing Myself
to the World—I Am Alicia ▪ Introducing Myself to
the World ▪ If I Were an Animal ▪ One Important
Time ▪ Self-Image ▪ Me Then ▪ Me Now ▪
Peak Experience ▪ How I Think Other People
See Me ▪ Plan for My Self-Image ▪ Self-Image
Mender—How I Would Like to See Myself ▪ Body
Image ▪ Body Image—Lindsay's Story ▪ Emotional
Mad (Sad, Glad) Lib ▪ Going Out ▪ Body Image
Exercise ▪ Voices in My Head That Tell Me I'm

Section III: My Feelings 139

Acknowledgments

This book contains many important voices. I want to thank my team of teen and young adult consultants for keeping these pages real and honest. Here it goes: Many, many thanks to Alex Dayton, David Murphy, Katrina Becker, Danny Stolzman, Megan Auster-Rosen, Richard Russell, Alissa Kronovet, Kamali Robinson and Ali Levine. Being with you was a high point of working on this book. I also want to thank Marina Dayton, Belinda Bellas, Heather Delaney, Olivia Zaleski and Kathryn Zaleski for their consultation and support, and also to my students at New York University for generously sharing their stories and insight in these pages.

My appreciation to David Rosenker, vice president of adolescent services at Caron Foundation in Wernersville, Pennsylvania, and New York City for consultation on the Self Test for Drugs and Alcohol. Julie DeVillars could not have been a more terrific editor for this book. She worked her magic everywhere. Many thanks to Lawna Patterson Oldfield, typesetter and cover designer for this book, who brought the pages and book jacket to life with style, creativity and her own special talent. Allison Janse, who followed the book through the production process with patient and penetrating attention to detail. Trish Roccuzzo, who prepared the original manuscript with professionalism and enthusiasm. Finally, warm appreciation to Christine Belleris, editorial director at Health Communications, Inc., for being her usual wonderful self and also an excellent editor.

Introduction

This is a book to help you explore your identity, to look into all the different and complex parts of you that make up who you are. Through this book, you will have the opportunity to decide what parts of your child self you want to take with you into adulthood and what parts you wish to revisit or release. Growing up is hard. Teenage years are transition years, when you are moving from childhood into adulthood, when you are constantly changing, constantly transforming. Walk into a teenager's bedroom and you might find anything from teddy bears to condoms. These years contain all of it.

Growing up includes a lot of changes and anticipation. When you're a kid you can't wait to be twelve, then when you're twelve, fourteen seems old, then sixteen, then eighteen, then you can't wait for the exciting and terrifying prospect of college. Each stage is a giving up of something and putting it into our bank of memories, our personal history of who we are so far and an adding on of something new. Each year can be like a decade in terms of how much you are changing. Your emotions can be all over the place; you might feel like your identity is moving in lots of different directions. Some days your sense of who you are is totally secure, and other days you can feel completely clueless.

Use this book as your own private place to explore who you are. Share it with trusted friends if you want to. Form an informal journaling group and talk about your experiences if you like. Keep it next to your bed, in your backpack for whenever you need it or simply for your eyes alone.

Journal Pages

The exercises in this book are ways to get your feelings out or to look at something in a new way. There is no doing them right or wrong—just do them in any way that works and is helpful and enjoyable for you. There are additional blank "process pages" at the end of the book. You can use these if you need more space for some of the exercises or if you want to do additional writing on your own.

A Word About Journaling

Journaling is like a personal free-write. Just put your pen on the paper and let your heart pour out. Don't worry about how it looks or sounds. THIS IS FOR YOUR EYES ONLY, unless you wish to share it with people you trust. Journaling lets you pour your feelings and thoughts onto the paper so you can get a better, clearer look at them, so you can let them unravel by themselves, so you can get them off your chest. Think of the page as a friend and let yourself talk.

Section I:

He who conquers others is strong;
He who conquers himself is mighty.

—LAO-TZU

When I say "I," I mean a thing absolutely unique,
not to be confused with any other.

—UGO BETTI

Inside myself is a place where I live all alone
and that's where you renew all your
springs that never dry up.

—PEARL S. BUCK

The spirit is the true self; not that physical
figure which can be pointed out by your finger.

—CICERO

To thine own self be true, and it must follow,
as the night the day, thou canst not
then be false to any man.

—SHAKESPEARE

T he most important relationship we will ever have is with ourselves. If we are on "good terms" with ourselves, if we treat ourselves well, talk to ourselves with kindness and respect in our own heads, we can lead comfortable and happy lives. We can stand by ourselves when we need strength, motivate ourselves when we need a push and love ourselves when we need a friend. When we're on "bad terms" with ourselves, we cut ourselves down from the inside and ignore our needs and inner voices.

Learning to be friends to ourselves is daily work. We need to watch our thoughts; are we being kind inside or mean to ourselves? We need to watch our actions; are we doing self-destructive things or acting in a way that is for our own good? We need to watch our feelings; are we paying attention to what we feel, listening to our inner voice and guiding it gently toward reason, or do we alternate between letting our feelings run us in any direction and pretending they're not there?

The journey of self is the most exciting journey in the world. When we get to know ourselves, to accept our own insides and work with them instead of run from them, we can become strong and healthy people. In order to do this we need to be patient, committed and responsible to and for ourselves. We need to care about ourselves the way we want others to care about us. We need to give ourselves a chance to succeed and get the help we need along the way. We need to have faith that life will work out.

This positive way of looking at things helps to give us choices. We can choose the type of life we want to live and the kind of people we want to be with and slowly take steps toward both. It starts today. It starts now. You are building the foundation upon which your self will grow.

Good luck, and enjoy the journey because the journey is the goal.

My Photograph

In the space below, paste a photograph of yourself. Choose a picture that speaks to you.

What do you like about this picture?

_____

_____

_____

_____

_____

What do you imagine you are thinking in this picture?

_____

_____

_____

_____

_____

Why were you drawn to this picture?

_____

_____

_____

_____

_____

How does this picture represent you?

_____

_____

_____

_____

_____

If this picture had a voice, what would it say?

_____

_____

_____

_____

_____

Is there anything about this picture you would change? If so, what? If not, why?

_____

_____

_____

_____

_____

Collages

Flip through magazines and find images, words and letters that feel as if they represent you, what you're all about and where you're going in life. Make a collage that's all about you in all your various aspects.

Introducing Myself to the World

I Am Alicia

Hi! I'm Alicia.
I am Alicia and I am intelligent.
I am attractive. I am creative. I am nurturing. I am caring.
I am independent.
I am the child of an alcoholic.
I am the grandchild of courageous people.
I am the daughter of immigrants.
I am an American.
I am part South American and part Slavic.
I am organized. I am neat. (Sometimes I am compulsively
   neat and organized.)
I am creative. I am multilingual.
I am a pretty good cook.
Sometimes I am lazy. Sometimes I'm driven.
Sometimes I push myself too hard, but I'm working on that.
Sometimes I'm a good listener. (Sometimes I'm not.)
I am curious. I am spiritual. I am traveled.
Sometimes I'm powerful. Sometimes I'm powerless.
Sometimes I'm scared.
Sometimes I am very brave.
I have herpes.
Sometimes I feel lonely.
Sometimes I feel inadequate.

Sometimes I'm a little girl. Sometimes I'm a woman.

I'm athletic. I like to write.

I am an aunt. I am a sister. I am a friend.

Sometimes I get lost.

Sometimes I feel overwhelmed.

Sometimes I feel sexy.

Sometimes I feel scared.

Sometimes I don't know the right thing to say and I get
   scared.

Sometimes I say things that I don't like later.

Sometimes I act silly.

I am a grateful member of an eating disorders group.

I am giving. I am generous.

Sometimes I worry what others think of me.

Sometimes I feel ashamed. Sometimes I feel guilty.

Sometimes I feel warm and snuggly.

Sometimes I feel hurt and angry.

I am a novice skier.

I am a fast learner.

I am a survivor of sexual abuse.

I have a strong will to live. Sometimes I lose that will to live.

Sometimes I feel proud of my accomplishments.

Sometimes I feel envious.

Sometimes I feel frustrated.

Sometimes I am determined.

I am complex. I am a package deal.

I come all wrapped up in many feelings and emotions.

I am Alicia and I'm glad to be alive.

I am who I am and I'm glad to meet you.

Who are you?

These are the top three strengths of my animal:

1. _____

_____

2. _____

_____

3. _____

_____

If this animal could introduce itself to the world, it would say:

_____

_____

_____

_____

_____

This animal's favorite activity is:

_____

_____

_____

_____

_____

One ImportAnt TiMe

Think of an age that was in some way important to you. What was it? (Use a picture if you wish.)

_____

_____

_____

_____

_____

Describe yourself at that time:

_____

_____

_____

_____

_____

_____

What would you like to say to yourself then, knowing what you know today?

_____

_____

_____

_____

_____

_____

Reverse roles: What would you like to say from the role of yourself at that time to yourself today?

_____

_____

_____

_____

_____

_____

What part of yourself from that age is still with you today that you treasure?

_____

_____

_____

_____

_____

_____

What part of that self is still with you today that you have let go of?

_____

_____

_____

_____

_____

_____

What do you know now that you wish you had known then?

_____

_____

_____

_____

_____

_____

Me Then

Paste or draw a picture of yourself from a few years ago or your childhood that speaks to you.

What were your worries?

_____

_____

_____

_____

_____

What was your most fun thing to do?

_____

_____

_____

_____

_____

What were your sources of pleasure or quiet contentment?

_____

_____

_____

_____

_____

What did you feel good about in yourself?

_____

_____

_____

_____

_____

What embarrassed you about yourself?

_____

_____

_____

_____

_____

When you look back at your family, what do you see?

_____

_____

_____

_____

_____

What was your school experience?

_____

_____

_____

_____

_____

Me Now

Paste or draw a recent picture of yourself that speaks to you.

What are your worries?

_____

_____

_____

_____

What is your most fun thing to do?

_____

_____

_____

_____

_____

What are your sources of pleasure?

_____

_____

_____

_____

_____

What do you feel good about in yourself?

_____

_____

_____

_____

_____

What embarrasses you about yourself?

_____

_____

_____

_____

_____

When you look at your family, what do you see?

_____

_____

_____

_____

What is your school experience?

_____

_____

_____

_____

PeaK EXperience

Look back on your life and try to identify a time when you felt that you were having a peak experience. A peak experience is any experience that had a profound and lasting effect on you. For example: beginning high school, a hiking trip where you climbed a mountain or visited a new country, a relationship that changed your life and perspective, a teacher who changed your life significantly, even a painful experience like your parents' divorce could be a peak experience when you deepen your understanding of life.

My peak experience was: _____

_____

_____

_____

_____

It changed my life in this way: _____

_____

_____

_____

_____

_____

It affected my thinking in the following ways:

_____

_____

_____

_____

It affected my self-image in these ways:

_____

_____

_____

_____

_____

I will never be the same in these ways:

_____

_____

_____

_____

_____

_____

_____

_____

_____

_____

_____

_____

_____

_____

_____

_____

HOW I THINK OTHER People See Me

My friends see me as _____

_____

_____

_____

_____

My mom sees me as _____

_____

_____

_____

_____

My dad sees me as _____

_____

_____

_____

_____

My brother(s)/sister(s) see me as _____

_____

_____

_____

_____

My teacher, _____, sees me as _____

_____

_____

_____

_____

Other teachers, _____, _____

see me as _____

_____

_____

_____

Teachers in general see me as _____

_____

_____

_____

_____

My relative, _____, sees me as _____

_____

_____

_____

_____

Other relatives see me as _____

_____

_____

_____

_____

Authority figures see me as _____

_____

_____

_____

_____

*That which oppresses me,
is it my soul
trying to come out in the open,
or the soul of the world knocking
at my heart for its
entrance?*

RABINDRANATH TAGORE

Plan For My Self-Image

1. What is the image you have of yourself?

_____

_____

_____

_____

_____

2. What image do you want to create for yourself?

_____

_____

_____

_____

_____

3. What things do you find yourself doing to create a certain image (maybe that you don't really want to be doing)?

_____

_____

_____

_____

_____

_____

4. What do you think you could do for yourself that would improve the way you think and feel about yourself?

_____

_____

_____

_____

_____

_____

Self-Image Mender

How I Would Like to See Myself

On this page make your self-image the way you would like it to be. Dream a little—let yourself play!

MY IDEAL SELF-IMAGE

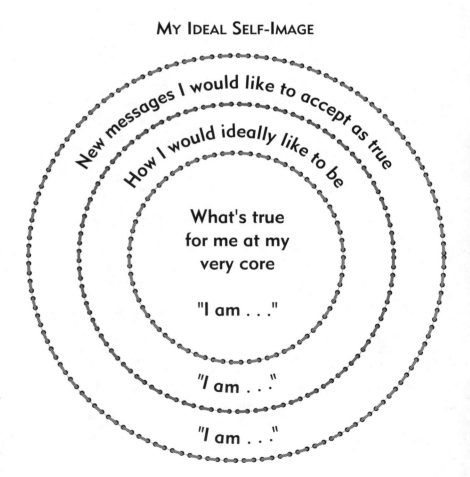

New messages I would like to accept as true

How I would ideally like to be

What's true for me at my very core

"I am . . ."

"I am . . ."

"I am . . ."

When I look at my new self-image this way, I feel _____

_____

_____

_____

_____

_____

The part that makes me nervous is _____

_____

_____

_____

_____

_____

The part that excites me is _____

_____

_____

_____

_____

_____

When my self-image is like this, I feel _____

_____

_____

_____

_____

_____

When my self-image is like this, I don't feel _____

_____

_____

_____

_____

_____

When my self-image is like this, I can _____

_____

_____

_____

_____

_____

BODy ImAgE

Be thin! Be fit! Be perfect! Get style! We are bombarded with hundreds of images a day telling us what we're supposed to look like in order to be okay. No one walks through normal life looking airbrushed all the time, but somehow the media makes us think we should—that if we don't there's something wrong with us. We are so overfocused on how we look that we're terrified to look in the mirror and be who we are. That's why so many of us have distorted body images—that is, we look perfectly okay but we feel as if we don't. We get down on ourselves for every bit of cellulite or for having less than perfect pectorals.

Be Thin!

What does this lead to? Poor self-image and maybe eating issues. Some of us would rather put our health at risk by starving ourselves or binging and purging to chase the fantasy of looking perfect than to be who we are. This is so tragic—it can lead us into a downward spiral or, worse, to the disease of eating disorders. Beauty is ultimately an inside job. It comes from within. We need to give ourselves a break from this crazy mania about looking perfect and cultivate some better values.

Be FIT!

Think about the people you love and admire in your life—the ones you would turn to with a problem or with whom you genuinely enjoy spending time. Is it their looks that you're responding to, or is it who they are on the inside? Developing the inner qualities that cre-

Get Style!

ate a good character gets you a lot further in life than ignoring your insides.

Research shows that it's not necessarily the most popular kids in school who do well in life. If you haven't taken the time and energy to develop inner strength, tolerance, sensitivity and goodness, then when you're on your own you don't have enough to fall back on. You need inner strength to hold you up, to keep you going. Looks fade, but character builds over a lifetime. *Our bodies are meant to house who we are, not be who we are.* It's great to want to look good and take care and pride in your appearance. But if you let it go too far and you think you are what you look like, that's sad and empty. And when you think about it, it's personality that mat-

Be Perfect!

ters. Someone with a great personality ends up looking good because their energy just comes through as attractive. In a very real way, beauty does come from within. Then we wear it on our faces, in our eyes and in the way we carry ourselves. That's the kind of beauty that grows throughout life.

BODY IMAGE

Lindsay's Story

I am insecure about the way I look. I worry constantly about how I look. I am always comparing my appearance to that of other girls. I have an intense fear of becoming really fat and having to shop in plus-size stores and never being attractive to guys. I often feel ugly and unworthy of affection from guys. I feel inadequate in relationships. I feel like my body is covered with a disgustingly excessive amount of fat.

I become really irritated by eating sounds. It bugs me to hear chewing noises and smacking of lips. I hate it when people eat on the phone. I find loud eaters to be revolting. I am especially upset when I see my mother overeat. I watch her put food into her mouth and it practically makes me sick. I want to pull it out of her hands and prevent her from consuming the fattening foods she devours. I want her to have some self-control and restraint.

Sometimes I lose control when I eat. I consume large amounts of food at one time and really fast. I feel like I'm in a trance when I do it. I do this when I'm alone. I keep it a secret. I then vomit violently until I get it out of my body. I really feel ashamed. I think my mother's overeating reminds me of my own weaknesses around food. Her shape also reminds me of how I might look if I eat too much. Then I'm reminded of what I am doing to prevent it—and I feel ashamed. My mother is a representation of the fat me I could become. The me I am terrified of. The me I hate.

I am constantly thinking of food, weight and fat. I can feel fat all over my body. I hate it. I hate the body you gave me, God. I don't understand why you did not give me a better body and a high metabolism.

I am terrified. I can just imagine what my mother thinks. "I am so lucky to have a handsome husband. He is so good-looking, but I am fat. He must want other women and not the fat cow that I am." She was thin when he fell in love with her. I remember my mom thin. She was happier. I want to be happy. If I don't get thin enough, I will be alone and unhappy for the rest of my life.

I am alone and depressed. I fill that void with food and then I purge so I won't get fat and be alone forever. I look in the mirror and see the gross ripples in my thighs. I see how huge the curves are. I am disgusted with the body you gave me. I am punishing the body you gave me to have another body, a better body.

In the next passage, Lindsay imagines herself without this issue in her life. She writes . . .

I am a healthy woman who does not worry about my body or my weight. I am happy with the size and shape you gave me, God. I trust that you have made me beautiful and I do nothing to change your design. I don't stress about food, calories or fat. I don't stress if I miss a day at the gym. I rarely feel ugly.

I am at a restaurant with friends. I eat the same size meal they do. I do not have a single thought of guilt. I don't sit there trying to figure out how I can get rid of the calories or how I can make up for eating it. I eat and just enjoy the company and the taste of the food you have given me.

I do not weigh myself every day. If I do weigh myself, I do not stress over one-pound or two-pound changes. I look in the mirror at myself naked and I see a beautiful woman. A woman who is natural and healthy. I love what you created in me.

EmOTiOnal
MAd (SAd, GlaDD LEb

When I look at myself in the mirror, I feel _____.

(adjective)

I like my _____ and my _____,

(noun)   (noun)

but I'm not so crazy about my _____ and

(noun)

my _____. When I think of other people

(noun)

looking at me, I feel _____. When I was

(adjective)

little, I liked to feel _____. Now that I'm

(adjective)

older, I feel _____. I think my friends

(adjective)

think my body is _____.

(adjective)

I do ❏ /don't ❏ agree with them. The opposite sex sees

me as _____. I see myself as

(adjective)

_____. When I look at other kids and

(adjective)

their bodies, I feel _____. One thing I

(adjective)

would like to change about my body is my _____.
(noun)

The way I can change it is to _____ and
(verb)

_____. My eating habits are
(verb)

_____. I eat _____ food.
(adjective)   (adjective)

I think the way I see myself is (different from ❏ / the same

as ❏) the way other people see me. It would be better if I

saw my body as more _____. I tend to
(adjective)

be _____ on myself. I do ❏ / don't ❏ accept
(adjective)

my body. I need to learn to be more _____.
(phrase)

Going Out

Brenda slides into her third outfit of the night; she looks beautiful. She stares critically into the mirror and turns away in disgust. "Why didn't you guys tell me how huge my butt looks in these pants?" Everyone looks at her in confusion. "Brenda, you couldn't look thinner, you aren't allowed to complain to us when you are wearing size-two pants."

"Yeah," Laura says. "Just stand next to me in the mirror and you'll feel much better. Now that is what I call big," she says, inspecting her own hips. Everyone gathers around the mirror to figure out who has the most reason to complain.

Our bodies surprised us at puberty. Each of us is equally dismayed when we stare into the mirror and realize that we have a woman's body. We still expect the boyish frame, uninterrupted by hips or breasts.

Brenda is still scrutinizing herself in the mirror and turns to her friends again. "If you were really my friends, you wouldn't let me out of the house looking like this. Come to think of it, you wouldn't let me out of the house at all." Brenda's older sister looks alarmed. "Honey, look in the mirror again," she says. "Not only are you not fat, you're way too thin. If you don't start eating more you're going to look sickly."

"I know what you're doing," Brenda says to her sister. "You want me to be fat, you're scared that I might be thinner than you."

Her sister looks confused at this, although she knows exactly what Brenda is saying. With all the time that we all spend scrutinizing our bodies, we come to know the attributes and faults of everyone's figure. We compare and we envy, whether it's one person's petite frame or another's large chest. Though we all know that you can't put the large chest on the slim little body, we still strive to create this ideal. No one could guess why we spend endless hours in these empty debates. Our destructive mentality is inherited from our mothers, from our culture.

I wonder to myself if maturity alleviates our anxiety about our bodies. Are we able to stare in the mirror and smile when we are twenty-five? Do we gain some respect for our bodies after we have children? I am discouraged, however, by a conversation that I had with my mother just this morning.

She walked into my room in a pair of tight-fitting pants and went directly to the mirror. "Liesha, I think I lost a pound, do you see it?"

"Well, Mom, turn towards me."

"Right in here," she said, motioning to her hips. "I think I might have gotten past that damn plateau in my diet. I'm losing weight again."

As I stared at her body, I found it impossible to focus on the size of her thighs. I looked at her stomach in awe at the thought that she carried both my brother and me between her small hips. I remember the comfort of climbing into her arms and leaning my head against her chest. I can't imagine anyone finding fault in this miraculous body. Instead, she still stares at her own reflection and sees only that she has five more pounds to go, and then five more, and then more.

My friends and I are now all huddled around the mirror. It's ten o'clock and we all know we are not going to get any happier about the way we look tonight. So we make a pact: The diet starts tomorrow. We may have called a truce with our negative images for the night, but we know inside that tomorrow we will begin the struggle with our bodies all over again.

Realistic, healthy changes that I can make so I'll feel good about my body are _____

_____

_____

_____

Stupid, self-defeating attitudes about my body I need to let go of are _____

_____

_____

_____

The things about other people that attract me most are ___

_____

_____

_____

The things about myself that I think are attractive are _____

_____

_____

_____

Voices in My Head That Tell Me I'm Not Good Enough

Life consists in what a man is thinking all day.

—RALPH WALDO EMERSON

All of us have voices in our heads sometimes that make us feel bad about ourselves. We say mean things to ourselves. Sometimes it is not the voices of others that have the power to harm us as much as our own *inner voices* that get in our way and make us feel bad about ourselves.

It is worthwhile to stand back for a moment and listen to the way you talk to yourself. What do you say to yourself if you haven't done a good job or you feel that you don't look good? If you've never taken the time to listen to those voices, you may be surprised at how harsh you are to yourself.

Where do these voices come from? Some of them are the internalized voices of our parents, other adults, siblings or school friends. Others are the unspoken criticisms and judgments that we fear the authority figures in our life are feeling toward us. Generally, if people feel good about themselves, they tend to feel good about those around them. People who regularly express negative feelings toward us probably are feeling that way about themselves. Over time, if we're not careful, we take in their attitudes as our own self-concepts. We believe their negative voices instead of the positive ones that are also out there when we let ourselves hear them.

Are these inner voices truly ours? Do they have our best interests in mind? Do we really agree with what they are saying?

We need to learn to work with these destructive voices, identify them for what they are and not let them define and control us. We need to create and nurture a voice inside ourselves that does not undermine our progress through life, but encourages our positive growth toward real self-awareness. We need to talk to ourselves in a "self-talk" that builds us up instead of tearing us down.

*Change your thoughts and you
change your world.*

—NORMAN VINCENT PEALE

TOUGH
Inner Voices

In the spaces provided, write the mean things that you say to yourself on the inside.

Circle one of the loudest voices. See if you can figure out where you originally heard it. Who has talked this way to you?

_____

_____

_____

_____

_____

What would you like to say to the person or situation where you first heard that voice?

_____

_____

_____

_____

_____

_____

What would you like to say to yourself about these voices now that you have identified them?

_____

_____

_____

_____

_____

_____

My Inner Face Versus My Outer Face

*When you make the two one,
and when you make the inner as the outer and
the outer as the inner and the above as the below . . .
then shall you enter the Kingdom.*

—The Gospel According to Thomas (Gnostic Bible)

As children, most of us were not afraid to let our inner selves show. But as awareness of the outside world increased, we learned to edit our insides to fit into our ideas of what was expected and accepted on the outside. Though this is a natural process, it can cause us to lose touch with our inner selves.

Children often use transitional objects—teddy bears, pacifiers, blankets, even their parents—to keep their connection with their inner worlds alive as they reach toward the outside world. Adults may use mood-altering substances such as liquor to connect their inner and outer worlds comfortably, but these artificial means do not allow them to achieve a true balance.

When we learn how to be comfortable with what is inside of us to work with ourselves in a positive way and to allow more of that person to shine through into day-to-day living, we become more truly independent and develop positive self-esteem.

Inner Face Versus Outer Face

Identify a situation in which you are experiencing some difficulty. Briefly describe the situation in the space below. (For example: My boyfriend broke up with me and is dating someone else.)

_____

_____

_____

_____

Now, in the left column, write words that describe how you feel on the inside. In the right column, write words that describe how you show your feelings on the outside. For example:

INSIDE FACE	OUTSIDE FACE
ANGRY	indifferent
HURT	Cocky

Now do yours:

INSIDE FACE	OUTSIDE FACE

What does this tell you about how your thinking, actions and feelings on the outside, relate to your thinking, actions and feelings on the inside? Are they in balance or at odds?

_____

_____

_____

_____

_____

What Is My Shadow Self?

Your shadow self is the part of you that you deny the existence of. Think of a person who is sickeningly sweet—so sweet that it is disgusting. Don't you feel they're covering something up, something they don't want you to see or even to see themselves? That's the trick—they're not just hiding it from you, they're hiding it from themselves. That's what makes it a shadow. It follows them around, they can't get rid of it. It's long and dark, but when they turn around to see it they can't find it—it's gone.

That's the shadow—the dark part of yourself you don't want to know about. It can be a good part or a bad part. Maybe we hide the part of ourselves that's successful because we don't want people to be jealous. Or maybe we hide the part that's envious because we feel it's bad. One way it can come out is through hate. The thing we hate most about someone else might be the thing we're afraid we are. Test it out in your head. Who really bothers you? Is there some quality in that person that you're afraid you have? Play with this idea in the exercise. Read the example of Lindy's shadow side and see what you think.

The ShaDOw

I am Lindy's shadow. Though Lindy may look great, I am her shadow and I feel self-conscious all the time. I scrutinize every bump on my body, every tiny blemish—and I come up short. I feel constantly insecure, and I wait for other people to criticize me, to identify the real me under the façade. I fear they won't like the real me. I fear I am inept somehow or not enough. All these ideas about myself make me feel anxious, and I hate that feeling. I feel myself spiraling downward into anxious negative self-talk, and that makes me feel worse. Then I need to pump myself up in phony ways, and I get so dependent on other people thinking I'm okay or cool or beautiful. I feel like the shadow me starts to have a life of its own, and it's not on speaking terms with Lindy's outside personality that gets shown to the world. I wish the shadow and the outside personality could be friends.

The Shadow

The ShaDow Self

In the shadow, write words or phrases that you feel describe the contents of your shadow self, the parts of yourself that you might attempt to deny or keep in hiding.

Where in your life do you feel that this shadow self emerges?

_____

_____

How does it get in the way of your relationships? How does it get in the way of your goals and dreams?

_____

_____

Who are the people you feel jealous of or that bug you?

_____

_____

Do they share any qualities of your shadow self?

_____

_____

Write a dialogue between you and your shadow self.

Me: _____

Shadow: _____

Me: _____

Shadow: _____

Me: _____

Shadow: _____

Me: _____

Shadow: _____

Me: _____

Shadow: _____

The Critic That Lives Inside Of Me and Keeps Me Down

Critic: Hi, remember me? How could you forget? I keep up a constant monologue in your head. I am your Critic, I am your Censor. I am the negative voice in your head that puts you down, makes fun of you, tells you that you can't do something. But don't you know, I'm doing it for your own good. Without me, you would make a fool of yourself or get a big head. You'd say something stupid or get laughed at. You'd let everyone see what a loser you really are. I'm only trying to protect you from being found out. When you make a goal, I have to remind you that you were just lucky. If you get an A on a test, again it was luck. Don't, for a minute, relax or rest on your laurels. The moment you do, you'll be unmasked and everyone will see that you are really a fraud.

It's a tough job I have. I must be on duty all the time. I protect you from embarrassment and pain. I keep you motivated. You're not as smart or talented or attractive or thin or funny or cool or creative as—as anyone else. I must always compare you to others. If your hair looks nice, I'll remind you that you look fat. If you get an A-, I'll remind you that it's not an A+. If you write something, I'll tell you it's not good enough for anyone to see. If you win a game, I'll remind you that it probably won't happen again. And if you like somebody and want to ask them out on a date—ha! They'll probably laugh in your face.

▼▼▼▼▼▼▼▼▼▼▼▼▼▼▼▼▼▼▼▼▼▼▼▼▼▼▼▼▼▼

My Personal Critic

W rite a dialogue between yourself and the Critic that lives inside of you. What does it say to you? Does it hold you back from doing things? What things?

Me: _____

_____

Critic: _____

_____

Me: _____

_____

Critic: _____

_____

Me: _____

_____

Critic: _____

_____

Me: _____

_____

Critic: _____

_____

Me: _____

_____

Critic: _____

_____

Me: _____

_____

Critic: _____

_____

Me: _____

_____

Critic: _____

_____

Silence Your Inner Critic

W ho are you helping by beating yourself up and putting yourself down? No one! When you do, you hurt yourself and you're a drag on the people around you. Dare to see yourself in a positive light. You tell other people how to see you by the way you see yourself. You tell other people how to treat you by the way you treat yourself.

Draw a picture or make a collage of yourself in a POSITIVE light. Use words and symbols to represent your good qualities.

Talk back to your critic.

Section II:

My Family and My Friends

Govern a family as you would cook a small fish
—very gently.

—CHINESE PROVERB

Happy families are all alike; every unhappy family
is unhappy in its own way.

—LEO TOLSTOY

Bringing up a family should be an adventure,
not an anxious discipline in which everyone
is constantly graded by performance.

—MILTON R. SAPIRSTEIN

The mother's lap is the child's first classroom.

—HINDU PROVERB

That energy which makes a child hard to manage is the
energy which afterward makes him a manager of life.

—HENRY WARD

Children know the grace of God, better than most of us.
They see the world, the way the morning brings it back
to them, new and born fresh and wonderful.

—ARCHIBALD MACLEISH

Children need models rather than critics.

—JOSEPH JOUBERT

Our families teach us how to be a person. They show us by their own behavior how to act. Generally, if our families are nice to us, we learn to be nice to ourselves and other people. If they're mean, we learn that too. Some of our strongest relationship bonds are with our families. In fact, this is where we learn what relationships are all about. A good family whose members know how to show love, set boundaries and enjoy each other is a great start in life. They are our role models. If our family members don't know how to do these things, it can cause a lot of pain. Then it's a good idea to look for good role models in other families where we can learn good ways of relating. All families have ups and downs, good days and bad days, strengths and weaknesses. Family is one of life's riches. A family doesn't need to be perfect to be good. You can take a closer look at yours in these pages.

Friends are great. They're the people who are going through what we're going through at the same time. Or maybe we have an older friend we can look up to and get advice from or a younger one we can be a kid with. Our friends are people we can hang out with, do fun stuff with, share our feelings with and get comfort and support from. Hopefully, they challenge us to grow as well as letting us just kick back and be ourselves. Friends are a huge influence on us. Because we want to fit in, we tend to become like the people we hang out with. Good friends can make a huge difference in our lives. They can make fun out of an ordinary activity—hiking, shopping, watching a movie, going out for coffee. If we're hurting, they can help us feel so much better, and when we're up it's twice as fun to hang together. Friendship is one of life's treasures.

My Photograph

In the space below, paste a photograph of yourself as a child. Choose a picture that speaks to you.

What feelings come up as you look at this picture?

_____

_____

_____

_____

_____

What strengths do you see in yourself in this picture?

_____

_____

_____

_____

_____

What part of yourself in this picture would you like to let go of?

_____

_____

_____

_____

_____

What changes have taken place in you since this picture?

_____

_____

_____

_____

_____

What do you feel your inner voice is saying in this picture?

_____

_____

_____

_____

_____

What would you like to say to yourself in this picture from where you are today?

❝

_____

_____

_____

_____
❞
_____

Photographs

Read "Kristen's Answers" (following these pages) for an example of the feelings photographs evoke.

In the space below, paste a photograph of yourself alone or with others that particularly speaks to you.

What feelings come up as you look at this picture?

_____

_____

_____

_____

What do you imagine the people (including yourself) are thinking?

_____

_____

_____

_____

_____

What do you imagine they would like to say?

_____

_____

_____

_____

_____

What would you like to say to yourself or to anyone in this photograph?

_____

_____

_____

_____

_____

Kristen's Answers

What feelings come up as you look at this picture?

The picture above is of my sister and me. I was ten years old and she was around twelve. As I look at this picture, I feel sad for the years that have gone by when we were never close. We never shared our feelings with each other. I also feel kind of sad that we might never be close. We were walking through the meadow, and I picked some daisies. Then she snatched the daisies out of my hands and threw them at me and laughed. When I think about what is going on in the picture, I get a feeling in my stomach. I guess I should laugh at what seems like a harmless joke. However, when I look more closely at this picture, I feel hurt, embarrassed and ashamed. I was more attractive and outgoing than my sister. I feel ashamed that friends and boyfriends came easier to me. I feel silly for picking and wanting to hold flowers. I feel ashamed for wanting to look pretty when she couldn't. I feel sad that she was lonely. I always felt weird about being more attractive than she was because she acted like I did something awful to her. Now I feel angry that I was the object of her anger, resentment and jealousy.

What do you imagine the people (including yourself) are thinking?

In the picture we are both smiling, but those are our masks for the camera and for the world to see. I imagine she is thinking, "I look so ugly and Krissy looks so pretty. I feel very uncomfortable and stupid posing for this picture. Kristen is the cute one, she is always the center of attention. I know if I take those flowers from her it will mess her up and embarrass her. I know that it will get a laugh."

And I could be thinking, "I hate her. I look like an idiot. She always makes me look stupid. She always embarrasses me. I will never trust her."

What do you imagine the people in the picture would like to say to each other?

If this picture of me could talk I think it would say, "Why? I didn't do anything to you. I know you have a rough life and I am sorry, but why do you have to make me pay for it? I don't hate you. I just want you to like me. I even try not to be the best so that you'll like me. I just want us to be friends."

I think Maggie would like to say, "I don't mean to hurt you. I don't even want to but I have to. You have it so easy. You have everything and I have nothing. You're pretty and nice and people like you. You don't even have to do anything and I feel like hurting you, but I really do love you. It's just not fair that you can have everything."

What would you like to say to yourself or to anyone in this picture now?

I would like to say to my sister now, "I have always felt guilty for being the kind of person you wanted to be. You're my big sister and I wanted to look up to you. I'm happy you're doing well in college. I'm almost looking forward to your coming home for break. I think maybe we can hang out and you can give me advice about school. I think I'll write you a letter and see if maybe we can become friends as well as sisters."

Feeling Love

T hink of times when you feel loved and appreciated. How does this feeling of love affect your thinking? How does it affect the way that you see yourself and the situation you are in?

A situation in which I felt loved was _____

_____

_____

When I feel loved I _____

_____

_____

When I don't feel loved I _____

_____

_____

I need _____

_____

_____

Emotional
Mad (Sad, Glad) Lib

When I am with my family, I feel _____.

(adjective)

The biggest feeling I have toward my mother is _____

(adjective)

_____ and toward my father is _____.

(adjective)

Whenever we _____, I feel _____.

(action word)   (feeling word)

_____ is _____. He/she is

(proper name of relative)   (adjective)

really _____ to me. I really love it when _____

(adjective)   (proper name)

_____ with me. I really hate it when _____

(verb)   (proper name)

_____ me. I'm glad my family is _____.

(verb)   (adjective)

I wish we were _____. When we _____,

(adjective)   (verb)

it makes me feel _____. On the other hand,

(adjective)

when we _____, I feel _____.

(verb)   (adjective)

Sometimes I wish my _____ was more _____
(proper noun)   (adjective)

to me. When I was little I liked to _____ with my
(verb)

family. It always felt so _____ when we _____
(adjective)   (verb)

together. Sometimes I worry that I am not _____
(adjective)

enough. The biggest gift or lesson I've gotten from my family

is _____
(phrases)

_____.

FAmily
MyThology

We can spend a lifetime trying to live up to myths that are *our family's attempts to explain itself to the world or to itself.* (Ideas about itself are a part of our family's self-image.) Let's look at what some of your family beliefs are.

Answer these questions or finish the sentences:

If my family had a motto, it would be

66

99

We believe the outside world sees us as _____

_____

_____

During quiet moments we feel _____

_____

_____

My family gives high praise to _____

_____

_____

The three strongest values held by my family are

1. _____

_____

2. _____

_____

3. _____

_____

In medieval times, families had a crest. Draw your family crest:

Who do you get along best with in your family? Your parents? brothers? sisters? grandparents? pets?

_____

_____

_____

Who do you fight with in your family?

_____

_____

_____

Is there anyone with whom you are not comfortable?

_____

_____

HINT: Some problems can be solved, some can't. Sometimes, if we can't solve the problem any other way, all we can do is find ways to connect with people outside the family who can give us support and guidance. Then we just need support in sharing our real feelings and getting involved with positive activities that make us feel self-confident and independent— like a job, school activities or a hobby. Remember: this stage of life is not forever. Enjoy it while you have it and, if you have some problems, think about how you would like your life to be in the future and make plans and take steps toward it.

What can you do to take care of yourself so that you feel okay or to help the situation if that's possible? For example, "Talk to a teacher I admire," or "Get a job," or "Find a hobby."

_____

_____

_____

_____

What are the ways I can act that make my family work best for me?

_____

_____

_____

_____

What are some activities I can get involved in that I enjoy and make constructive use of my time?

_____

_____

_____

_____

Letters To My Parents

A Letter to My Mother

Each of us has two parents. Our parents are the most important people in our childhood. They affect us in every way: good, bad or indifferent. In these pages, write a letter to your mother and one to your father saying any and all of the things you wish to say, need to say, never said, wish you had said. *You will not give or mail these letters to them.* Even if you don't know your parent, write to the parent you don't know—they're still real for you. These pages are for your eyes only, for your heart to speak. (Use more paper or the process pages at the back of the book if you need to.)

A Letter to My Mother

You've Got Mail

Dear Mom,

Love,

A Letter to My Father

HIdden FAmily Messages

In the space below draw a picture of you and your family or paste any photograph you have that moves you, speaks to you or seems to have a hidden story.

Next, make two balloons (like the ones in comic strips) for each person. In one write what the person is thinking and in the other what (s)he is saying and fill them in as you see fit.

Example:

Meeting Parents' Expectations

Ryan's Story

My mother expects me to be the smartest guy in my class and to get straight A's. When I came home psyched because I got a ninety on a test, she asked me what happened to the other ten points. She tells me she is so proud of me, but I know that she really expects more of me. I feel as though my whole life has been mapped out for me—go to a good school, go to law school, be successful. I want to want things for myself, not because my mother wants them. . . .

Finish Ryan's story. Write how you imagine he might feel. Write how he might work toward his own goals or find ways to satisfy himself and still keep his relationship with his mother.

_____

_____

_____

_____

_____

FAmily Exercise

I n the box below, paste or draw a picture of your family that represents a time or incident that stands out in your mind (for example, the family on vacation). Look at the picture for a while. Below the box write what you see and/or feel when you look at the picture. (Use extra paper if necessary.)

This Is What I See When I Look at This Picture

_____

_____

_____

_____

Changing Places

Pretend you are another person (sibling, friend or parent) and answer these questions about yourself from their perspective:

a) What is your favorite thing about _____?
(fill in your name)

_____

_____

b) What do you dislike about _____?
(fill in your name)

_____

_____

c) What about being a family member/friend of _____
(fill in your name)

_____ has been hard for you?

_____

_____

d) What has been easy about being a family member/friend

of _____?
(fill in your name)

_____

_____

e) What do you envy about _____?
(fill in your name)

_____

_____

f) What role does _____ play in the family?
(fill in your name)

_____

_____

g) Do you feel close to _____?
(fill in your name)

_____

_____

h) What would you like to say to _____?
(fill in your name)

_____

_____

Learning by Imitation

My Parents' Divorce

N ote: Divorce can be tough on kids. It can leave you wondering what went wrong and if it has anything to do with you. It can also make you feel insecure about your own potential relationships. But you can work through these feelings and learn from them. Then you are in a position not to make the same mistakes your parents made. You can be the designer of your own relationships. Read Amanda's story for more information.

Amanda's Story

Thinking about my parents' "relationship" leaves me with empty images. They separated when I was two years old, so as far as I'm concerned, they were never really together. I don't remember them as a couple, and I don't remember my father living in our house. Photographs of my parents from the past seem fake, as if they posed for the pictures so that they would eventually have proof—proof of something that never really existed. I learned the word "divorce" when I was six years old.

I have no memory of my parents showing any love for each other. They just fought and fought. Everything was about money. Money, money, money. Of course, other problems came up over the years, but most of the fighting was over money. Petty and silly. Stupid but safe. I learned words like "alimony," "custody," "sue."

If my parents' relationship had a voice, what would it say?

It would say, "I'm sorry . . . I'm sorry that you don't believe I was ever good. I'm sorry you didn't get to know my good side better. I'm sorry you only saw me when I had turned sour. I wish you could have seen me when we laughed together, traveled together, hugged each other and loved each other."

What would this voice say to me?

"I'm sorry that you have to sit here today writing about me as a painful memory. I'm sorry that I didn't have better gifts to leave you. I'm sorry that you are crying as you write this. I'm sorry that I couldn't set a better example for you and your future relationships. I'm sorry that I caused you to worry about money all the time. I'm sorry I caused you to feel so isolated from your friends who had parents who were married. I'm sorry. So, so sorry."

The lessons I learned about relationships and intimacy from my parents have only recently become more clear. Obviously, they were not great role models in the love department. I learned that love can fail, that it can end, and that "living happily ever after" is not guaranteed when two people fall in love. I learned to fear relationships, yet I desperately crave them. Relationships and intimacy are mysterious to me, since I never witnessed either between my parents. It is difficult to really know what I learned from my parents about relationships and how it has made an impact on me in my relationships. I think that a lot of what I learned from my parents' relationship is tucked away in my subconscious. Only when I started to pursue my own relationships, like my first boyfriends, did these "lessons" surface. I am still trying to understand some of these stored fears about relationships. Perhaps that is the key to the feeling of mysteriousness behind relationships for me — my parents did not provide me with lessons on love, but rather fears. It is quite common to fear the unknown.

What I want from my own relationship someday:

I would like a partner I can be open and honest with. I would like us to support each other in each of our separate lives and dreams, then come together to share love, time and each other.

I want to be realistic. No one can "save" me or make my life work. I have to do that myself, but I want someone to share the journey with me.

I have faults and my partner will have faults. I don't want to be perfect in order to be lovable, and my partner will not have to be perfect either.

I want us to share common goals and values and to work together to create a good life.

My FAmily DiagrAm Example

Use these symbols to represent your family members. Use circles to represent females and triangles to represent males. Draw yourself and your family members to show how you see yourself in your family. Pay attention to the size and location as you draw the circles and triangles to best represent their relationship to you. Are they close or distant, big or small compared to you? Look at Trish's diagram for an example.

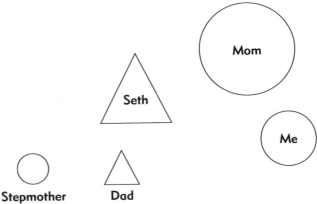

When you look at your symbol, how do you feel? *Okay, but a little too small compared to Mom, a little squashed.*

Is there anything you'd like to change or wish were different? *I'd like to be bigger, I'd like Mom to be smaller, I'd like to be closer to Dad.*

Now, do your "wish" diagram: Redo your diagram the way you would like it to be.

TRISH'S WISH DIAGRAM

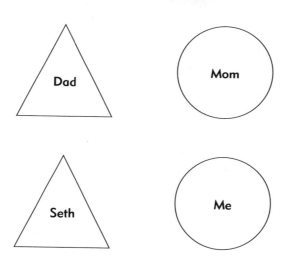

My FAmily DiagrAm

Use these symbols to represent your family members. Use circles to represent females and triangles to represent males. Draw yourself and your family members to show how you see yourself in your family. Pay attention to the size and location as you draw the circles and triangles to best represent their relationship to you. Are they close or distant, big or small compared to you? Look at Trish's diagram for an example.

When you look at *your* symbol, how do you feel?

_____

_____

Is there anything you'd like to change or wish were different?

_____

_____

Now, do your "wish" diagram: Redo your diagram the way you would like it to be.

MY WISH DIAGRAM

How did your position change in both size and relationship to others?

_____

_____

How do you feel when you look at those changes?

_____

_____

How would you move your relationships?

_____

_____

Whom do you feel too close to in your original diagram?

_____

_____

Whom do you feel too far away from in your original diagram?

_____

_____

Why is the "wish diagram" a better setup for you?

_____

_____

_____

_____

_____

FAmily Poetry

Soliloquy—
(Some Unfinished Business I Have with My Father)

by Stephen

I feel lonely
I feel separate from you, from my body, from the world
I want to be more accepted by you,
less judged.
I want the freedom or is it permission
to walk less tenuously
in the thin air we breathe and share.
I feel sad that I feel scared
of you, of rocking the boat.
Sometimes I don't even know which
boat we are on, which body of water
we rest in.
Sometimes I feel washed ashore, by the
waves of your energy,
water rushing me,
I am drowning.
I am struggling to breathe, to see, to feel,
to live
with you and without you.

Write your own poem to your parent:

_____

_____

_____

_____

_____

_____

_____

_____

_____

_____

_____

_____

_____

_____

_____

_____

A LOOK
from Heaven at
My FAmily

Alyssia's Story

My name will be Alyssia and I will be born in about four years. Looking at you sitting with each other, I'm not sure where I will fit into this picture. I am scared that maybe you don't want me. That your family is full and by the time I come you will be tired and just won't have anything left to give. Maybe you are all happy just the way you are? It looks like Kelly and Dad have paired off and Mom and Tyler are happy together. I am afraid I won't fit in. Mom, you look so pretty and soft, I wish I could be sitting on your lap right now. Why do I have to wait? I wish I could play with Kelly and Tyler now when they will be closer to my age. Just looking at you makes me feel like an outsider looking in. I feel really alone and I want to fit in. You're all sort of smiling but don't really look comfortable. It almost looks like Mom and Dad aren't going to let the camera really see them, see what's really going on. And Dad, you look so far away. Tyler, you look like fun and like you would be a really nice older brother to have. And Kelly, you seem happy as if you are in the middle of a giggle.

I wonder why, Dad, you don't have your arm around Mom or why Tyler and Kelly are not on your lap. You aren't touching each other. There seems something posed about this picture. It feels like I can't really see you. I so desperately want to see you. I so desperately want to be hugged, and I'm not even here yet. But what if there is just no more love left? I will love you all so much. I will look up to you and I will try to make everything up to you. I will try to give you back everything you lost.

If you let me come into your family, I promise to be a good girl. I won't bother anyone. I'll try to fulfill all your needs because I can feel that Mom and Dad have been through a lot of pain. I'm not perfect, but I'll try to be if you'll just love me and accept me. I won't ask for much, I just want to belong, to find a place in your family and in your hearts.

Twenty-One Years Later

Well, I was born and here I am, a seventeen-year-old. Looking at this picture reminds me of this ideal of the perfect family that my family wanted to be so desperately, but it is a picture and not the reality. It was like a sinking ship. We would just patch the hole and pretend we weren't all dying. Oh God, I loved all of you so much when I was born. All four of you seemed like superhuman beings. Kelly, you were seven years old. Tyler, you were eleven. You were both like my second parents and you were both more available to me than Mom and Dad could be. But that must have been hard taking care of me, when you were both so young and needed care.

It is unbelievable how this photo captures the entire family dynamics. Mom and Tyler were so close. And I adored both of you and felt like I was most like you. Everyone commented on how much the three of us looked alike, fair and tall. I always felt jealous, Kelly, that you were Dad's favorite. You guys seemed so similar, you were the "good girl" and I ended up being the "wild child." You did everything that was acceptable to Mom and Dad, except your two marriages. Kelly, you seemed so perfect just like Dad, you were neat, quiet, worked hard, saved your money. Both of you were never late and never made mistakes. It strikes me how alike and different we are at the same time. How differently and individually all of that unresolved pain from depression and Dad's alcoholism shot through all of us. I know that before I was born I promised to be your healer, and I am truly sorry I let you down. I know now I can't heal you. I know now that the only one I can heal is myself. I am still plagued with guilt, as if I left you all on that sinking ship.

FAmily GOds and GODDesses

Close your eyes and think of those things that are idealized in your family. They might be work, popularity, brains, success, athletics, beauty, power, money, failure and so on. These are your family's gods and goddesses. Now, using symbols or words, represent or describe these various gods and goddesses in your family in the box below.

Now try to figure out which family member(s) worship(s) the different gods and goddesses. Write their names next to the word or symbol.

What gods and goddesses do you want to keep, and why?

_____

_____

_____

_____

_____

_____

Which ones do you want to let go of, and why?

_____

_____

_____

_____

_____

_____

GODS
and GODDesses

A Journal

In the space below, write a journal entry in the first person of one of the gods or goddesses from the previous exercise, Example: "I am the Goddess of Beauty. I live through Mom's dreams. She worships me through hairdos and clothes and plastic surgery. She wants her daughter, Chloe, to worship me, too. But Chloe hates to shop!"

I am the God(dess) of _____, I . . .

_____

_____

_____

_____

_____

_____

_____

The GOOd STUff

Write down the name of a family member:

_____

Finish the following sentences about this family member:

A nice thing _____ does for me is: _____

_____

_____ _____

Something we have in common is: _____

_____

What makes me smile about _____

is: _____

_____

My favorite thing to do with _____

is: _____

_____

Write down the name of a different family member:

_____

Finish the following sentences about this family member:

A nice thing _____ does for me is: _____

_____

_____

Something we have in common is: _____

_____

What makes me smile about _____

is: _____

_____

My favorite thing to do with _____

is: _____

_____

PeeⓇ PreⓈⓈuⓇe

Where Do I Fit In?

Sometimes I think it's too much to ask of anyone to be closed off every day with only people of your own age. The pressure builds. There is maximum school time together, plus after-school activities, then evening and week-end social life and minimum time for yourself and your family. Then you feel out of it if you're not with someone, so you hardly get any time alone just to kick back and relax, just to be. Part of our peer pressure is overexposure and messages from T.V. that are constantly telling us we need to fit in.

Peer pressure has a few strong effects. It can make us do things we wouldn't normally do just to belong—giving up our own better judgment or our own sense of right and wrong. We may adopt what is called a "mob psychology" and do whatever the group is doing. Peer pressure can also make us hide parts of ourselves that we feel the group might reject or make fun of. The down side of this is that we don't develop certain sides of ourselves that might help to round out our personalities, actualize our potential or strengthen our character. If the values of the group are not good, we can be encouraged to grow in negative directions, hate other people, use drugs, be violent or have a screw-the-world mentality. If the values of our peer group are good ones, pressure from the peer group can encourage us to grow in positive directions, to feel good about who we are and excited about our lives. Positive pressure could

include Outward Bound-type experiences, community serv-
ice, developing artistic sides, genuine interest in learning, care
for other people and the environment, or just hanging out and
having a good time together. The kids we are with help to
shape the adults we will one day become. The friends we are
with are powerful models for us. Peer groups can motivate us
to do all sorts of great things if we're with good people. They
can be our greatest source of friendship, support, fun and challenge. They can get us to stretch in all sorts of wonderful ways.
They are the people we grow up with and share our hearts,
thoughts, clothes and fun with. They are our friends.

Feeling Chosen. We all want to feel chosen, noticed, seen,
appreciated. In group dynamics the kids who are chosen most
often get chosen even more, so the most energy or choice goes
toward the fewest people. Groups act that way in any situation.

Alex

*I am really popular. I don't mean that to sound stuck-up, it's
just the way it is. I'm in the "In" group. I got voted on school
council and I didn't even do anything. I'm sure I'll be on the
homecoming court. I wear cool clothes. I never once rode the
bus; even before I had a car someone always offered me a ride
home. I guess a lot of people want to be like me.*

*I know someone reading this might say, "Well then, what are
you complaining about?" But I feel like I'm in the spotlight. I
am always stressed out. I feel like I have to act a certain way all
of the time. I mean, I spend more time worrying about what I
am going to wear to school to look cool. People expect me to
look good so I have to, right? And I have to be seen at the right
parties, so sometimes my homework has to slide. I can only go
out with certain people. I mean, if I hung out with someone*

who was less popular than me, people would be like, "What's up with that?"

But, it's like, I'm really good at bowling. I make it seem like my parents drag me to go with them, but I secretly like to bowl. But of course that isn't cool. I mean, me on the bowling team at school? I don't think so. I mean, I ran into someone from my class at the alley once and I had to make a big deal about how my parents had forced me to go and wasn't this embarrassing, ha, ha. And look at these dorky shoes I have to wear. And then I had to act like I wasn't having fun in case she saw me.

So, it's kind of sad in a way. I mean, they see my clothes and the way I look and the way I act and they admire that. They want to hang out with me, but they don't know the real me. I know this sounds weird, but they only want to hang out with me because other people want to hang out with me.

Actually, not being highly chosen can be fine if you have *enough* kids choosing you. Sometimes being highly chosen is being *over-chosen*. Kids aren't choosing you for you, but because everyone else is choosing you—so it's not really you they're choosing, but an image. Having fewer choices that are more real and sincere can actually feel more secure sometimes. We all play more than one role. Which one do you identify with?

Exploring Roles

The Hero or Superpopular Person. This person tends to embody the qualities that the peer group most values: qualities that the media, friends, parents or teachers make us think are the most important. What are those qualities?

_____

_____

_____

Which qualities do you think are important? Which are superficial?

Important: _____

_____

Superficial: _____

_____

The Scapegoat. The scapegoat (nerd, freak) tends to embody those qualities that members of the peer group reject, don't want to have or are worried they might have but reject in themselves. What are those qualities?

_____

_____

_____

_____

Which of those qualities might be desirable in an adult (for example: studious and responsible)?

_____

_____

_____

The Rebel. Rebels tend to act out opposing qualities from those that authority figures or even some peer group members value. They are rebelling *against* the status quo. There can be a piece of the rebel in all of us, so the rebel acts out something we may feel, too. Sometimes the rebel acts out the negative feelings their peers don't feel comfortable expressing. But they get stuck in the role and get their sense of power in a negative way. What are ways your peers rebel? Which ways might be harmful?

_____

_____

_____

_____

The Clown. The clown provides comic relief. When there is tension in the group, the clown cracks a joke to break it. Or the clown might say what's on everyone's minds—but what no one dares to say—in a funny way and everyone knows what they mean and feels relieved. What is the good side of being a clown? What is the not-so-good side?

Good: _____

_____

Not so good: _____

_____

The Peacemaker. The peacemaker is the person everyone feels they can talk to, who really "understands." What is the good side of being the peacemaker? What is the not-so-good side?

Good: _____

_____

Not so good: _____

_____

The Invisible One: The invisible one is the person who just blends in, who no one notices very much. What is the good side of being the invisible one? What is the not-so-good side?

Good: _____

_____

Not so good: _____

_____

What's Happening in Your Peer Group?

SUPPORT. We all need support in order to feel connected to other people. It's natural and it's important. Who supports you?

_____

_____

IDENTIFICATION. We need to have people we can identify with who like to do what we like to do and have values similar to ours. With whom do you identify?

_____

_____

COMPETITION. Competition is normal. We need to learn to use competition to stimulate us to grow in ways that we want to grow and to take on new challenges, instead of making us feel as if we'll never be best, so why try? With whom do you compete?

_____

_____

_____

RIVALRY. This one can be tricky. Some people bring out our primitive characteristics like hate, gossip and meanness. Some of this is okay, but we need to see it for what it is and not get stuck in it. Who are your rivals?

_____

_____

_____

CHOOSING. Choosing is really important. We all make choices constantly, and we need to learn to make choices that are good for us—that lead us down good paths. Do you feel comfortable speaking out about choices when you are with your group? If no, why not?

_____

_____

_____

BEING CHOSEN. We all need to feel chosen by somebody. It gives us a sense of being recognized as something good. We also need to learn to be comfortable being chosen or seen. Whom do you feel chosen by?

_____

_____

REJECTION. Most of us feel rejected by someone somewhere along the line. It can be tough to live with if we take it too personally. Whom do you feel rejected by?

_____

_____

INTIMACY. Most of us have people we feel we can trust and open up to more than others. With whom do you feel you can open up to and share who you really are?

_____

_____

FUN. Some of our friends are chosen by us because they are especially fun. Even if we don't feel that trusting or intimate, we like to be with them because they're fun. Whom do you choose for fun times?

_____

_____

My Friend DiAgram

U se the symbols of circles to represent girls and triangles to represent guys. First locate yourself on the page in whatever size and location best represents how you see yourself in your group. Next, locate your friends in whatever size, distance or closeness that best represents their *relationship to you*. Label them with names or initials. Example:

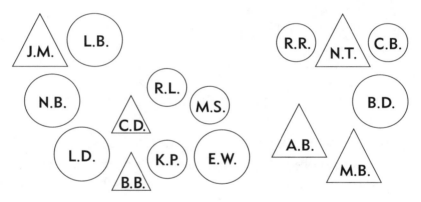

Now do yours:

When you look at your symbol, how do you feel?

_____

_____

_____

_____

Is there anything you'd like to change or wish were different?

_____

_____

_____

_____

▲●▲●▲●▲●▲●▲●▲●▲●▲●▲●▲●▲●▲●▲●▲●▲●

Now, do your "wish diagram." Redo your diagram the way that you'd like it to be.

How did your position change in both size and relationship to others?

_____

_____

_____

_____

How do you feel when you look at those changes?

_____

_____

_____

_____

How would you move your relationships?

_____

_____

_____

_____

Whom do you feel too close to in your original diagram?

_____

_____

_____

_____

Whom do you feel too far away from in your original diagram?

_____

_____

_____

_____

Why is the "wish diagram" a better setup for you?

_____

_____

_____

_____

Journal—Friends
finish this...

At school there are lots of "cliques" or groups of friends, and sometimes I wish I could just hang out with anyone I like, not just the people I'm "supposed" to hang out with.

Sometimes I . . .

_____

_____

_____

_____

_____

_____

_____

_____

_____

_____

_____

Friends

Emotional Mad (Sad, Glad) Lib

Most of my friends are _____. Sometimes
(adjective)

I feel like I have _____ friends. I think my friends
(adjective)

are a _____ influence on me. The major ways
(adjective)

they influence me are _____ and
(phrase)

_____. Sometimes I feel
(phrase)

_____ from, (or than) my friends. I worry
(adjective)

that they see me as _____. I know they
(adjective or noun)

_____ me. It's really important to me that
(verb)

my friends know I am _____. The thing I like
(adjective)

best about my friends is that they are generally _____.
(adjective)

But I wish they were more _____ sometimes.
(adjective)

I think my friendship group is _____. Some
(adjective)

of my friends feel _____ and others feel
(adjective)

_____. _____ gives me
(adjective)   (proper name)

a pain in the neck.

My closest friends are _____, _____.
(proper names)

My friends who are a good influence on me are _____,
(proper names)

_____. _____, _____ aren't
(proper names)

such a good influence on me. I would like to get to know

_____ better.
(proper name(s))

My friends mean a lot to me because _____

_____
(phrases)

_____

_____

_____

_____

_____

Being Me in a Time Of Conformity

You're a teenager. It's a time when trendsetting is taboo. Going with the flow is the only form of acceptable behavior. How do you maintain a sense of yourself? In a time when black and white are the only two options, how can you express your true colors? Where does personal expression come into play? Adolescence can be a difficult battle between our growth into our adult selves and the influence of our peers to "fit in."

Think about the following statements:

There are those who seek themselves in others and cripple their own individuality and creativity in the constant search for acceptance. And then there are those whose excessive attempts to be different lead to a friendless life of solitude.

Last, there are those who fall somewhere in the middle, seeking acceptance of others while still allowing who they are to shape themselves.

Where do you fall?

_____

_____

How do you feel about where you fall in?

_____

_____

_____

_____

_____

_____

Is there anything you want to change?

_____

_____

_____

_____

_____

_____

A Q&A on Friends

Does dressing a certain way make you a certain kind of person?

What things have you done that you didn't want to do but everyone expected you to?

A Q&A On Friends

(continued)

Are all of your friends supportive of you?

Do you surround yourself with people who respect you for who you are, or do you have to be someone you're not?

A Q&A on Friends
(continued)

Are there some people you hang out with who do not deserve your trust?

Do you ever feel as if you are playing a certain "role" in your group of friends/ the people you hang out with?

Are you comfortable with your role?

Personal Power

Do you give away your personal power by constantly worrying about what other people think of you—if you're in/out, cute/not, popular/out of it, smart/dumb, etc., etc., etc.?

You give away your power when you constantly obsess about what's going on outside of yourself and you forget to drop down into your own heart and look for peace, calm and sustenance there. You are entitled to your fair share of internal power. It's not arrogant to feel empowered or good about yourself—it's claiming your piece of what everyone shares. It doesn't mean power against someone else. It means allowing yourself to be all you can be and drawing on your own inner pool of strength.

Let yourself say in your mind whenever you like, "I have a right to my own power, to my own vision of life."

Section III:

My Feelings

Seeing is believing, but feeling's the truth.
—Thomas Fuller, M.D.
Gnomologia

*The important thing is to be capable
of emotions, but to experience only one's own
would be a sorry limitation.*
—André Gide
Journals

*All the knowledge I possess everyone else can
acquire, but my heart is all my own.*
—Goethe
The Sorrows of Young Werther

*In a full heart there is room for everything,
and in an empty heart there is
room for nothing.*
—Antonio Porchia
Voces

*The head does not know how to play
the part of the heart for long.*
—La Rochefoucauld
Maxims

Talking Out Feelings Versus Acting Them Out

Sometimes we just can't find the right words to describe what we feel. As a matter of fact, we can't identify the feelings either. Our inner world is no different from any other space. If we ignore it for long enough, things pile up and pretty soon we can't find anything. So we slam the door shut on our insides and hope that one day we'll open it and it will have magically cleaned itself. Or we wait until it gets so full that the door will burst open, and it will be an obvious mess. And maybe then we get the message and start sorting.

Nicole's parents are getting a divorce. It's been in the air forever, but now it's really happening. She doesn't want to talk about it. It's hard to talk about because she feels embarrassed. Also she thinks talking won't change anything, so why

bother? She doesn't want to "go there." She's not even sure
what she's afraid of, but she is sure that if she talks about it,
she'll feel bad. Also, talking about it just makes it too real, and
right now it feels unreal as if she's watching a movie of her
life—as if this isn't really happening. So she withdraws, stiff-
ens her upper lip (and the rest of her body) and trudges on.
One of the most traumatic and upsetting events of her life
goes unspoken.

What do we feel we are gaining by this type of emotional
silence? Why? What are we afraid of losing if we open up? We
might be sitting on huge emotions that we fear letting go. We
imagine that they will immobilize us. We think that if we don't
speak out about them, they will somehow lose power within
us. But just the opposite is the case. Emotions that are not
talked through gain power. Think about it. It's true.

If we don't talk out our problems, we are at risk for acting
them out. In the beginning it might be hard to talk about
because we're sort of numb and whatever is happening doesn't
feel real yet. At that point our pain might leak out without our
even knowing it. Upset about her parents' divorce on a deep,
unspoken level, Nicole yells at a friend for dropping her
books. Carrying the pain of a morning fight with his mom,
Andy overreacts to a situation at school. Desperate from a lack
of parental love and a stable home, Jeremy brings a gun to
school and shoots his pain at an unsuspecting student. Emotional pain does not magically disappear—it needs to be spo-
ken, talked out, shared and heard. Otherwise it comes out in
our actions. It gets acted out, and we aren't really aware of
what we're doing. It is not necessarily the trauma itself that
produces a lifelong wound, but the fact that it was never talked

about. When stress, trauma and emotional hurts are held in silence, they grow inside of us. Talking releases the hold they have on our insides. Talking allows us to understand what we're feeling. Talking lets us put it somewhere in our heads that makes sense, instead of having it sit inside of us like a heavy stone that doesn't move. The message is clear. Talking about your feelings is good for your health.

THe TeeNagE BraIn

Did You Know . . .

R ecent brain imaging studies actually show that teen-agers' brains work differently from those of adults. Teens use the *amygdala* to process information more than the *cortex*. The amygdala was formed earlier in our evolution and is more instinctual and emotional than the cortex, which evolved later and is associated with planning, reasoning and moral judgment. Teens act differently from adults because their brains operate differently.

When teens get triggered they may get emotional or impul-sive and have a harder time becoming reasonable, settling down and seeing things in the long term. This can make someone feel overwhelmed with strong feelings that make situations hard to think through. Just understanding this can help us be patient with ourselves until we settle down inside and see things clearly. Feeling emotions strongly can be excit-ing and wonderful as well as scary. It's all part of getting to know ourselves and life.

EVER WONDER WHY IT'S HARD FOR TEENS TO PLAN AHEAD?

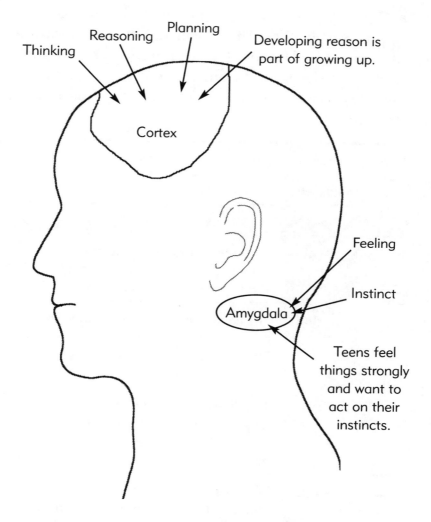

Thinking

Reasoning

Planning

Developing reason is part of growing up.

Cortex

Feeling

Instinct

Amygdala

Teens feel things strongly and want to act on their instincts.

Learning to think things through and attach words to feelings leads to emotional literacy.

Button Pushing

Sometimes we get our buttons pushed by someone or something. When this happens, we need to take a moment and figure out what is being triggered. Why am I suddenly reacting so strongly either inside or outside? Is some old hurt getting pushed on and leaking into the present situation?

What Button Is Getting Pushed	What's Getting Triggered from Another Time
EXAMPLES:	
Anger	The time Liesha took Scott away from me. Now when I see her flirting with Todd, that old anger is triggered.
Hurt	The time I got left out of Kelsey's birthday party and everyone said it was so great. That's getting triggered when I see those guys eating lunch together.
Criticism	The times my dad criticizes me for all sorts of little things. That hurt is getting triggered when my teacher asks me why my homework is late.
Low Self-Worth	When I see the cool kids laughing together, that feeling that I don't really belong anywhere since my parents' divorce gets triggered.

Write Your Own:

_____

_____

_____

_____

_____

_____

_____

_____

_____

_____

_____

_____

_____

_____

_____

_____

_____

_____

_____

_____

_____

DiAlOgue wiTh a wOunDed Aspect Of Self

On this page, write your own dialogue between two parts of yourself. For example:

Trevor: Hey, why are you hiding out and dissing anyone that tries to be nice to you?

Wounded Part: Josh and the other guys don't treat me with respect. I can feel it, and I feel bad and stupid inside.

Continue back and forth. . . .

_____

_____

_____

_____

_____

_____

_____

_____

The Development Of Myself

Think about a time in your life when you were sad, lonely or in pain. How old were you? _____

Go to that age in your imagination.

Pretend you are that age. Write a journal entry about yourself (e.g., I am twelve or nine, etc., my name is _____ and I . . .).

_____

_____

_____

_____

_____

_____

_____

Examples

I am Teresa at thirteen. I am worried because my sister is sneaking out to be with her boyfriend.

I'm Aaron. I'm eight. My parents are fighting. I'm scared of divorce.

I'm Vanessa at sixteen. I went to school today and no one talked to me.

_____

_____

_____

_____

Write a poem about yourself at that time.

> *Lonely*
> *Because nobody likes me*
> *anymore.*
> *They laughed at me*
> *and said why*
> *would they hang*
> *out with a*
> *freak?*

_____

_____

_____

_____

_____

_____

_____

_____

Write a letter to someone from that time. Express your real feelings—what you weren't able to say to them then.

Dear _____

Example

Dear Courtney,

I hate you! You were supposed to be my best friend and you stood there with Eileen and laughed at my outfit. What did I do wrong?

Your ex-friend,
Vanessa

_____

_____

_____

_____

_____

_____

_____

_____

_____

_____

_____

Next, reverse roles with the person you wrote to. Write a letter to yourself from them that you would like to receive.

Dear_____

Examples

_____

_____

_____

_____

_____

_____

Dear Van,

I am so, so sorry. I was feeling insecure and when the popular girls included me I couldn't resist. Even if it meant not talking to you. But I missed you! I regret it now. That was stupid, you were a true friend.

Love, Courtney

_____

_____

_____

_____

_____

_____

Decisions

Write about a period in your life that you feel was a decision time, significant in shaping who you are today. Describe yourself at that time in the third person.

Example

He was fourteen. He wanted excitement. His parents told him not to hang out with those guys, but hey—what they don't know won't hurt them, right?

_____

_____

_____

_____

_____

_____

_____

Did you make the right decision?

_____

_____

_____

What should you have done differently?

_____

_____

_____

Introducing a Wonderful Person

Go to a time in your life when you felt especially good about yourself. Pretend someone else is introducing you. Have them describe the good qualities that you have.

This is _____
who is _____
_____
_____
_____.

I also like _____
because _____
_____
_____
_____.

Em🅾TI🅾Nal AuT🅾bI🅾gr🅾ph🅈

Example

An emotional autobiography is not based on the real facts or how a situation actually was but how it felt on the inside, how it felt emotionally. Sometimes just telling about the way it was doesn't really do it—it doesn't get to the real experience and how we experienced the situation. Things may have looked one way but felt another.

In the following example, Jose lives in Tennessee but is of Puerto Rican descent. Sometimes it feels as if he's living in both places at the same time.

I'm Jose-Jo and I am growing up in a small, Latin country in the middle of America. Inside my house I live in Puerto Rico, and outside I live in Tennessee. I think and feel in two languages and they don't always match. Sometimes I feel in Spanish and talk in English. I get confused, and I don't know how to act or feel or make sense of things. I don't know what's expected of me because the rules keep changing. Living in two countries at the same time is weird sometimes. I feel some days like I belong everywhere and some days like I belong nowhere.

Emotional Autobiography

My name is _____

_____

_____

_____

_____

_____

_____

_____

_____

_____

_____

_____

_____

_____

_____

_____

_____

Mouse Girl

Heather's Story

Hello, I'm Mouse Girl. I live in a tiny hole in a house. I only come out of my hole when I have to. I'm afraid of the cat in the house. She's mean and tries to catch me. She is my enemy. If she sees me, I freeze and stay very quiet. I stay out of her way. Otherwise, she pounces. I look forward to becoming a bigger mouse so I can move out of my mouse hole and not be afraid in my own house. As a mouse, I feel safe in a corner but when I come out I have to scurry and sneak before I'm seen. I feel like no one sees me and when I open my mouth I feel like only little squeaks come out. I like watching and I see a lot of things other people miss. Sometimes I feel cute and little and sometimes I feel gray and dull. I don't know how to get bigger. I worry about being stepped on if I come out.

Animal Me

C hoose an animal you feel has qualities similar to yours. Describe yourself and your situation from this perspective, using "Mouse Girl" as an example.

_____

_____

_____

_____

_____

_____

_____

_____

_____

_____

_____

_____

_____

_____

_____

Uhat Do I Do with Sadness?

Running away from sadness—hiding from it—doesn't work. Pretending that we're always happy is phony. When something upsetting happens it's normal to be sad, in fact it would be a problem if you couldn't be sad. It would mean you were out of touch with your inner truth—that you weren't able to understand your own feelings.

When really big things go wrong like your parents getting a divorce, someone you care about dying or losing a close, important relationship, sadness is more than a passing feeling. Then it becomes grief. Then you actually need to go through some emotional stages to get through it to the other side.

Surprisingly enough, the first stage is **numbness**. It's that feeling that this really isn't happening. I'll wake up and everything will be the same as it was—no feeling—everything seems unreal. It's hard to talk about what happened because it hasn't really sunk in . . . we're numb. Then the next stage is called **yearning and searching.** That's when you have a pain in your heart or an ache in your gut. You want back what you lost or something like it to replace it—to fill up the empty hole. The third stage is **disorganization, anger, despair.** Everything feels different, weird, not like it's supposed to be and makes us mad—then despair comes, as if it will never get better, no matter what. Then the fourth stage is called **reorganization**. That's when our life begins to reorganize itself and we feel okay again. Not the same, but still we go on. Most of the time, if we get through it, we feel much stronger and understand a lot more about life and ourselves because of our experience.

The important thing with sadness and grief is to accept it, feel it and let it run its course. We will get to the other side if we don't try to pretend it doesn't exist. Some things that happen when we deny it are: we play tough, we drink and drug to kill the pain, or we get stuck in disorganization, anger, despair and our lives get really thrown off track. We can't seem to get motivated or back on course. We're constantly being pulled down by our own insides.

Facing problems and working them through is what makes us grow and become stronger and more self-confident. Running from problems does just the opposite—we get fearful and insecure. Here are some exercises to help you work with problems you may be having. Remember, problems in life are normal—they're part of being a person. It's what you do with them that makes the difference between growing or shrinking.

NOTE: *In the following pages we're going to explore all aspects of the grief process from anger to sadness to depression and loss. Some feelings have to do with loss, some are just a normal part of every day life. Check it out.*

Emptiness

Eric's Story

Sometimes I feel sad for no reason. I have great friends. I do well in school. My parents love me very much and will give me things when I ask for them. I don't know why I feel such an empty place in my heart. I wonder if it is from my relationship with my sister. Maybe it comes from my bad breakup with my girlfriend. What I need to know is if this emptiness is within me just because that is what I am. I sometimes try to fill the space by partying. At the same time I want things to be better at my base, at the bottom of my personality.

Maybe this emptiness is just a space that I need to fill with new skills, adventures, demanding more from myself. Maybe I need to take happiness as a momentary event rather than an ideal state of being (that's what my father has told me from his life perception). He says it's normal not to be happy all the time—nobody is, it's a feeling that comes and goes several times a day. Either way I need to fix this dissatisfaction with life. I need to be in love with myself. I need to know that I have a good heart, I am a good person, I deserve good things and I have time to learn more about how to be happy from within. This seems to be the purpose of life at this moment.

Being MAd

I am mad at _____

The reason I am so mad is _____

_____

_____

_____

I can't believe they would _____

_____

_____

I'm afraid they'll _____

_____

_____

It really hurts me because _____

_____

_____

If I could say anything I want to them, I'd say _____

_____

_____

_____

I wish I could change _____

_____

_____

_____

If only they hadn't _____

_____

_____

_____

They also hurt me when they _____

_____

_____

_____

The part that makes me feel powerless is _____

_____

_____

_____

The part where I feel powerful is _____

_____

_____

_____

What I hate the most is _____

_____

_____

_____

If I could change anything it would be _____

_____

_____

_____

What Is Anger?

*A man that studieth revenge keeps his own
wounds green, which otherwise
would heal and do well.*

—FRANCIS BACON

Anger is bad, right? Not really. First of all, let's talk about some useful purposes of anger. Anger gives us information that we can use if we take the time to feel it and figure it out. Anger can tell us something is going on that we need to pay attention to. Often what is going on is that our feelings are hurt. We then have a choice. Do we tell someone that we have been hurt by their actions? Or if they aren't the type we can share our true feelings with, do we act out? Sometimes we are angry if we think someone has treated us unfairly. Can we pause long enough to process our angry reaction and turn it into a meaningful communication with the person we're mad at? Or do we burst, get mad and alienate the very person we actually need to communicate with? Even if we can't talk our anger over with the person we're mad at, we can still talk it over with someone else, examine what we're feeling and work our way into a better place.

Acting Out and Acting In

There are different ways in which anger can be shown. *Acting out* ways might take the form of being sarcastic, hitting someone, ridiculing them, whining and/or manipulating.

Acting in is when we turn anger inward against ourselves. We become depressed, beat up on ourselves, mutilate ourselves, develop eating disorders, use drugs, drink alcohol, withdraw from others. When we act in, we deny ourselves pleasure, good feelings and positive experiences.

Past Anger Versus Present Anger

Unresolved anger from other past situations can get mixed up with anger in the present. Anger feels confusing, overwhelming and unmanageable. Then we are in danger of *acting out* or *acting in* in destructive ways. We need to figure out the past anger and resolve old wounds so the anger that comes from old wounds doesn't keep leaking out today.

One clear signal that we're carrying old anger is if we are feeling more anger than a current circumstance merits. For example, if you were hurt by a father who was constantly critical of you, do you tend to overreact to criticism at school? In other words, does criticism become a hot button that, when pushed, makes you react with anger that causes you to *act out* or to *act in?* If you have extreme reactions to everyday hurts and disappointments, you might have unresolved hurt from the past. Working with that past hurt rather than running from it can provide relief and insight. You can understand and learn from past wounds. By doing this you can reduce the powerful grip your anger has inside of you.

How Much Anger Is There?

Then there's the question of the amount of anger. Is anger a commodity like flour or sugar that builds up over time and that, with help, we can empty out like a trash can or a storage bin? Or is it something we create over and over again in the present? Or is it some of both? The first task becomes how to resolve old anger that may be influencing your current thinking, feeling and behavior. Next, you reshape new attitudes and practice new behaviors that will allow anger to be used constructively so it doesn't build up over time and get too big to handle.

Stay Out of Fight, Flight, Freeze

When we get triggered into historical anger, old anger is getting mixed up with current anger and we might fall back on early defenses. Think of a dog who has been yelled at—he freezes, growls or runs away (freeze, fight or flight). That's a normal fear/anger reaction for both people and animals. When we get stuck in fight, flight or freeze, we can't think straight or sort out our conflicting emotions. Instead of thinking through our anger, we just react or stuff it. Sometimes all we need to do is be aware of our angry feeling, think a little about it and let it be.

On the next pages you will find some ways of working with anger that might help you to understand and manage it. Remember: We all feel anger, that's normal. It's what we do with it that makes the difference in how it affects us.

Dealing With Your Anger

Time Out. Take a break when you feel yourself starting to get madder than you want to.

Breath Awareness One. Even out your breath by breathing in slowly through the nose and letting out slowly through the mouth.

Breath Awareness Two. Breathe out short, quick breaths through the mouth.

How Important Is It? Keep the big picture in mind; will this matter in five years?

Reverse Roles. Pretend you're the other person and try to see the issue for a moment as they see it.

Reality Check. Is your angry response larger than the current situation merits? Is there something else bugging you that makes you overreact to this situation?

Look at the Options. Try to avoid getting locked into a rigid or defensive idea of what the outcome of a conflict should be. Stay out of fright, flight, freeze.

Expect Minor Conflicts. Life will not be conflict-free. Expect conflicts and learn to deal with them effectively instead of overreacting to them or pushing them away.

Don't Catastrophize. Don't make things worse than they are by letting yourself run wild in your reaction.

Don't Get Stuck in Blaming. Blaming another person over and over again can keep us stuck.

Avoid Playing the Victim. You may feel victimized, but try not to get stuck in seeing yourself as a victim. You have choices and personal power.

Dealing with Anger Before the FAct

Meditate. Through daily meditation we allow the mind to "rest" and deepen our sense of spirituality.

Relax. Through daily relaxation we calm our breathing and bring our nervous systems into balance.

Good Nutrition. By eating healthfully we get adequate fuel for energy and avoid foods that throw our systems into chaos.

Positive Thinking. Positive thoughts affect our overall mood and even our health.

Play. Play gives us time to be creative, to relax, to laugh and to lighten up.

Rest/Sleep. Deep sleep and REM (rapid eye movement) sleep allow the body to rest and the mind to "clean itself."

Exercise. Exercise is a major stress reducer. It produces feel-good chemicals in our bodies that counteract anger.

Enjoy Close Relationships. Intimate, supportive relationships that include a friendly touch produce chemicals that bond and relax us. We all need this to reduce our sense of isolation and calm ourselves.

Get an Interest. Be a joiner and a contributor. Find constructive, creative and/or challenging ways to channel your energy in positive directions.

Attitude. Turn a situation around and around in your mind like a kaleidoscope until you can get the right light on it.

How to Separate Yourself from Your Anger

Allow yourself to think about a situation that has happened in the past month in which you got too pissed off. Imagine the situation just as it happened. Pay attention to the point at which you became overheated.

In the space below, write words and phrases that describe your feelings at the moment you felt your anger was out of control.

EMOTIONS:

What was it that got you angry? How did you feel when you got angry?	What did you want to do?	What went on inside your body?
_____	_____	_____
_____	_____	_____
_____	_____	_____
_____	_____	_____
_____	_____	_____

How did your angry response change the way you were thinking?

_____

_____

_____

_____

How did it change the way you were feeling?

_____

_____

How did it change the way you acted?

_____

_____

How did you feel about the person or situation that made you angry? What did you think to yourself about that person? What beliefs contributed to your anger (i.e., he/she *should* have; I *should* have; etc.)?

_____

_____

_____

_____

_____

_____

_____

_____

_____

How can you look at the situation so it doesn't bother you so much? Recognizing that ultimately you have no control over another person, what can you do to keep yourself in a comfortable place?

_____

_____

_____

_____

_____

_____

_____

Letting My Depression Talk

NOTE: *Sometimes depression is seen as anger turned inward. In this dialogue, you hear the voice of depression open up from both sides.*

Depression talks to you:

I am Depression. As you know, I play a very big part in your life. I come and go as I please. I know that you are trying to live without me. I am so strong and powerful that it is very, very hard for you to get rid of me. In fact, I can't even imagine being wiped out altogether.

Let me describe my brute strength and force. I am a powerhouse. When I team up with Sadness I am especially fierce. You cry a lot . . . and you don't know why! It's because we come in and ruin your fun. I don't like you succeeding too much. I don't even want you to have too much happiness in any area. I guess it's because I'm just so good at being Depression! I am so very much stronger than Happiness. You hardly know the happiness feeling. You used to when you were a kid. But now I'm taking over! Happiness is only fleeting—I stick around.

Now I know you try to get rid of me. Lately, you cry so much. Boy, do I know how to do my job. I not only get you upset over your own life, but I also make you upset over other sad things going on in the world. Okay, even I'll admit some of this other stuff is truly sad. But I make you *cry* over it and let it carry over into your life! When you hear about people getting cancer or about wars in other countries, you cry and feel this horrible sadness. When you met a dog in your neighborhood that was very sick, you were so sad you could hardly carry on for a few minutes. I mean, I am powerful Depression, but accompany me with Sadness and POW!—I am *Hercules!*

As Depression I show myself in different ways. I used to make you tired a lot. I also love to show up during PMS time. I notice I come when you are at your weakest.

I mostly show up sometimes because of certain situations. There are many. Whenever something isn't going the way you think it "should," I come at you.

Hope

I am *not* Depression. I am something else, and I just need to have more power over it. Depression and I are separate, even though we often mesh together and feel like one thing. I will now try to watch it more and notice when I'm vulnerable and be ready to push Depression away.

As far as Sadness goes, it isn't terrible. I think it feels good to express emotion. I thank the universe for allowing me to be compassionate and caring toward others and able to express it so that I'm not left stuck with pain inside.

Talk Back to Depression:

Excuse me, Depression, but just who do you think you are? You think you are so important to my life. You think I need you to survive? Well, you're wrong! In fact, I'm so tired of you! I'm sick of you! Yes, we had a long relationship. Well, I'm going to sever those ties now. Oh . . . you think you'll stick to me like glue when I'm happy or trying to be? Well, you are *so wrong!!* I deserve to be happy. Big-time happiness! I don't need Depression. I'm going to succeed whether you like it or not. You're much smaller than you think you are. I am much bigger and stronger than you! When I feel you coming on, I will fight against you like an army. So long, Depression. I am working to completely wipe you out, and my goal is to push you so far out of my life that I don't even recognize you. I know it's okay to be sad once in a while, but happiness is going to prevail!

Write your own "Feeling Dialogue." First, talk *as* the feeling, then talk as *you* back to the feeling. Use the Process Pages at the end of the book if you need more room.

_____

_____

_____

_____

_____

_____

_____

_____

Loss Of a Person

L et's explore the impact of the loss of a person. The loss can be to death, divorce or separation of parents, a breakup, a friend who moved away or whatever feels like a loss. You can also do this exercise if you feel you have lost a part of yourself, like the fun part, the happy part, the secure part or maybe you didn't make a team or get something you wanted.

Who or what did you lose?

_____

_____

_____

_____

_____

How did you lose this?

_____

_____

_____

_____

_____

What was happening in your life when you lost this?

_____

_____

_____

_____

_____

Where were you?

_____

_____

_____

_____

_____

What were you not able to say then that you would like to say now?

66 _____

_____

_____

_____

_____ **99**

What are the treasures that you keep with you from this relationship or activity?

_____

_____

_____

_____

What is something that you carry from the relationship or activity that you would like to let go of?

_____

_____

_____

_____

Write an epitaph for this loss, or a short poem or paragraph. (An epitaph is something written as last words describing a person or written on a tombstone.)

_____

_____

_____

_____

_____

The DeaTh of My Friend

Justin's Story

By the time I got out of the hospital, I was confused, sick and weak. My leg surgery did not let me think beyond the medication and searing, shattered bone pain coming from my left knee. Occasionally, I would just yell "This sucks!" No other words were as adequate. I knew what had been drawn from me and the future that was drawn for me. Approximately twelve to sixteen months of physical therapy, which would be painful.

I was not in any way prepared for the news of my friend's death. My mother, crying, came to me and told me that Juan had died in the accident. Stunned and stoned on codeine, I felt nothing. Not because I was stoned, but more because I couldn't believe the concept of Juan not being alive. I cried for a few hours and forgot. I feel guilty that I forgot about it. Codeine, high fever and sleep blurred my thoughts of Juan and the image of a mangled car into something a little too surreal to mourn over.

Then I let the thoughts fade under thoughts of rehab for my leg and making up schoolwork and all that. About a month later, I received a memorial card of Juan, a picture of him as I remembered him, smiling. The poem printed on the picture was in Spanish. When translated, the poem was simple, leaving one phrase ingrained in my mind, "When we meet again."

The card triggered a whole feeling of mourning. For the first time, I was afraid of death. More and more I got angry, frustrated, not able to attend the burial or memorial services. Crying over little things became a big part of my life, but one that I could not share with anyone.

Eleven months later:

I still feel the same pains. There is still no place nor people with whom I can grieve. I think this was my biggest mistake. I did not take the time for myself to really grieve. Now I find myself searching for a mental and spiritual place to put my grief. I find it in small moments sharing stories of Juan and in going to the places we had been together, just for the sake of grieving. The rest is still to come. Waiting or ignoring it isn't going to help. I'm ready to talk about it.

L O S S

L oss is a part of everyone's life. We need to learn to deal with it so we can work it through and move on. In the empty box on the next page write in a loss that you are currently focusing on (i.e., loss of a friend; a breakup; death of a loved one; parents' divorce, etc.). On the lines stemming from the box write words or phrases that describe how you feel about the loss or what changes have taken place. Here's Ben's Loss Chart:

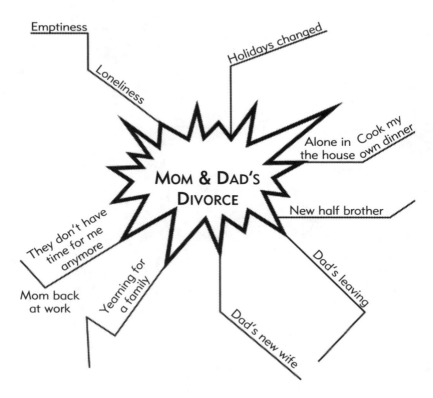

Personal Loss

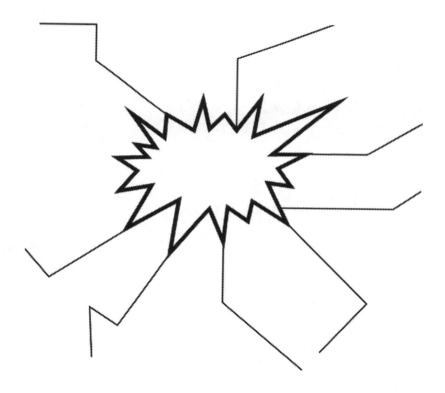

NOTE: *You can see from Ben's Loss Chart that one loss might have many little losses or changes attached to it. If we understand what they all are, it's easier to "get the full picture."*

ExAmining
a Loss

T hink of a loss in your life and answer these questions honestly.

	1 pt. none	2 pts. not too much	3 pts. some	4 pts. a lot
1. How many unsorted feelings do you still have about the loss?	❏	❏	❏	❏
2. How disruptive was this loss to your daily routines?	❏	❏	❏	❏
3. How much depression do you feel?	❏	❏	❏	❏
4. How much yearning and wishing for things to be the way they were do you feel?	❏	❏	❏	❏
5. How much emotional numbness or shut-down do you feel?	❏	❏	❏	❏
6. How much sadness do you feel?	❏	❏	❏	❏

	1 pt. none	2 pts. not too much	3 pts. some	4 pts. a lot
7. How much anger do you feel?	❏	❏	❏	❏
8. How much fear of the future do you feel?	❏	❏	❏	❏
9. How much trouble are you having organizing yourself?	❏	❏	❏	❏
10. How uninterested in your life do you feel?	❏	❏	❏	❏
11. How tired do you feel?	❏	❏	❏	❏
12. How much do you feel emotionally blocked or unable to express feelings around this loss?	❏	❏	❏	❏
13. How much regret do you feel?	❏	❏	❏	❏
14. How much do you beat yourself up or feel it's your fault?	❏	❏	❏	❏
15. How much shame or embarrassment do you feel?	❏	❏	❏	❏

Scoring the Examining a Loss Chart

Add up all of the points that your answers total.

✓ If you have fifteen to twenty-seven points, you are having a moderate amount of sadness.

✓ If you have twenty-eight to thirty-six points, you have a manageable amount of grief related to your loss.

✓ If your score is from thirty-seven to forty-five points, you are carrying quite a bit of sadness related to your loss.

✓ If your score is from forty-six to sixty points, you are carrying very much sadness related to your loss.

✓ If your score is anywhere between one and thirty-two or so, your emotional pain is within a manageable range. We all feel pain around loss to some extent.

✓ If your score is between thirty-three and sixty, it might be a good idea to try to get some help in dealing with this loss. Look around for an adult you can trust to open up to, maybe a parent, relative or friend, or try a school counselor or a therapist. You don't have to handle this alone. Sometimes just reaching out and breaking the silence can really help.

Mourning a Person

Think of a person in your life you have lost. This person might have died, left you or moved away.

Name the person: _____

Describe the situation as it was before the loss happened:

_____

_____

_____

_____

_____

Think of something about the relationship that had special meaning for you:

_____

_____

_____

_____

_____

What part of yourself did you feel you lost, along with the person that you lost, that you need to get back?

_____

_____

_____

_____

Describe what you feel might have been if it weren't for the loss:

_____

_____

_____

_____

In the space below, say good-bye to this person in whatever way feels appropriate:

_____

_____

_____

_____

_____

_____

_____

In the space below, say good-bye to yourself from this person. Reverse roles with them in your mind and write as them to yourself:

_____

_____

_____

_____

_____

_____

_____

Do you wish to thank this person for being in your life? How? Tell them:

_____

_____

_____

_____

_____

_____

_____

Stress

Stress is a huge problem today. Our lives are so busy and we try to do so much. We don't take the time to chill and enjoy life, to be with ourselves and our friends and family. Life isn't a race. It's a process. If we really don't take the time to look around us and appreciate the little things, we'll never learn contentment. We'll just be constantly trying to get this new thing or that new friend, thinking that then we can finally be happy. But happiness is here and now. It's just being content, appreciating what's around us and accepting ourselves and our lives. Stress is bad for your health. It makes everything worse than it really is, whether that's a cold or giving a speech or going to a party. A lot of stress we create in our minds. Uncreate it! Look at things from a different perspective. Will stressing over something really make it turn out better? Afraid not!

Next time you're about to have a stress attack, try this: Sit back, breathe in and out *slowly* a bunch of times and ask yourself, "Do I really need to stress over this or can I just relax and let it happen?"

Emotional Mad (Sad, Glad) Lib

I get so stressed out when _____ tells me to
(proper name; noun)

_____. Whenever he/she _____,
(verb)   (feeling word)

it makes me _____. I can't seem to let go of
(feeling word)

feeling _____. Maybe if I just _____
(adjective)   (verb)

him/her, I wouldn't be so _____. Another
(adjective)

thing that stresses me is _____. I take it so
(noun)

seriously. The voices in my head say _____
(phrase)

and _____ whenever I think about it.
(phrase)

When I look in the mirror I just want to _____.
(verb)

When I get really stressed out, I _____.
(phrase)

I think I would feel better if I could _____
(phrase)

_____.

Maybe doing less _____ and more _____
                  (noun or verb)   (noun or verb)

would help. I guess the things that I get the most stressed

about are _____, _____
                    (noun)   (noun)

and _____. The next time I feel myself
         (phrase or verb or noun)

beginning to get stressed, I will _____ and
                                              (verb)

_____ before I go nuts. Maybe being
            (verb)

more _____ with myself will help me
                (adjective)

feel less inclined to feel pressured. After all, in my case I think

I usually feel stressed because _____

_____

_____.
                            (phrase)

So I guess that next time I feel stressed out I'll _____

_____.
                            (phrase)

Stress Chart

List, in order of impact on your life, six things that stress you out, from most to least. Put them in the appropriate column.

Example:

Really stresses me out	Kind of stresses me out	Stresses me a little
1. breakup		
2.	school	
3.		zits
4.		
5.		
6.		

Now rate them along the graph above as to the level of stress you experience around them. Then choose one of the stresses and put it in the center circle below.

In the other circles write people, places and/or things that are a part of the stressful situation. (Choose the appropriate size and relationship to you in the center.)

What do you see about your stress chart that surprises you?

_____

_____

_____

_____

What aspects of this chart make you feel stressed?

_____

_____

_____

Which aspects do you feel hopeless about?

_____

_____

_____

Below write suggestions that you can make to yourself to make the situation feel less stressful:

_____

_____

_____

_____

Write Your Own Affirmations

Allow yourself to take a caring and close look within yourself.

What are your negative attitudes about yourself?

_____

_____

_____

_____

_____

_____

Where do these attitudes hold you back and block your life?

_____

_____

_____

_____

_____

_____

Write your own affirmations. No one knows you as well as you do. No one knows where you hurt as clearly as you do, or knows what attitudes need changing. First write one of the negative attitudes you wrote above. Then write the affirmation that you need to hear to turn that negative attitude into a positive one. For example:

My inner attitude: No matter how hard I try, I will always look ugly. Affirmation: My beauty comes from within me. Each day I invite Beauty to shine through in all I do.

Continue to write affirmations regularly and repeat them to yourself throughout each day.

_____

_____

_____

_____

_____

_____

_____

_____

_____

_____

Numbing Your Feelings

One of the ways we protect ourselves against feeling emotional pain is to numb our feelings. The problem is, while we're numbing out our painful feelings the good ones get numbed out, too. Pretty soon, we start to feel sort of dead inside. Though it can be scary to feel upsetting emotions, we need to remember that we can survive our own feelings. *Feelings aren't facts.* They come and go. Numbing them or shutting them down only *seems* to work. But underneath they nag at us, or leak out somewhere else. Feeling them, sorting them out, sharing and working through them means we can learn, grow and get closer to ourselves and other people.

One of the ways we may try to make painful or uncomfortable feelings go away is through drugs and alcohol. Drugs and alcohol work for the moment to quiet down upsetting thoughts that make us feel bad about ourselves or others. But while they are getting rid of our emotional pain, they are getting rid of our reason, too. In a sense we "lose our minds." When we use drugs and alcohol in this way, to control and manage emotional and psychological pain, we don't learn how to manage it on our own. Then we start to rely on drugs and alcohol to do what we should be doing for ourselves. Learning how to manage and work through problems is part of what makes us mature and strong people. Drugs and alcohol, when we abuse them, keep us from growing into who we can be.

Drinking & Drugging Self-Test

1. Do you drink? ❏ Yes ❏ No
   How often? _____

2. Do you do drugs? ❏ Yes ❏ No
   How often? _____

3. Why do you drink and/or do drugs?
   (Check as many as you like.)
   ❏ To be cool   ❏ To feel good
   ❏ To fit in with friends   ❏ To get rid of pain

4. Do you drink and do drugs when   ❏ Yes ❏ No
   you are sad so you'll feel better?

   If so, what are you sad or upset about?

   _____

   _____

   _____

5. Do you have a favorite drink or drug? If so, what is it?

   _____

   _____

   _____

6. Do you plan times when you can get high?   ❏ Yes ❏ No

7. Have your grades or school attendance dropped and/or your interest in school and school activities decreased since you started drinking and/or drugging?   ❏ Yes ❏ No

8. Have you changed your group of friends since you started drinking or drugging?   ❏ Yes ❏ No

9. Do you find yourself wanting not to be a part of family events a lot of the time since you started drinking or drugging?   ❏ Yes ❏ No

10. Are you becoming increasingly defiant with parents, teachers or other authority figures?   ❏ Yes ❏ No

11. Do you sometimes take things or do you sell things in order to get money for alcohol or drugs?   ❏ Yes ❏ No

12. Have you had any legal problems related to drugs or alcohol, like driving under the influence?   ❏ Yes ❏ No

This is a self-test to get you to reflect on your drug and/or alcohol use. If you answered yes to three or more questions on numbers four through eight, you may have a problem. The best thing to do is talk to someone who understands drinking and drugging—like a doctor, a therapist, your school counselor or a clergy person, or check out an open AA meeting.

My Story

Write a journal entry about your personal experience with drinking and/or drugs. Include any experiences where you used them or were around people who were using them. Include how it made you feel and what you observed.

_____

_____

_____

_____

_____

_____

_____

_____

_____

_____

_____

_____

_____

Party Girl!

Amanda's Story

I used alcohol and drugs to make my world better. I wanted things to be different. I read a word in a book that describes what I was looking for—transcendence. Right idea, wrong way of getting there. I wanted to be closer to God, and pot made me believe I was getting there. When I smoked, I was beautiful. When I drank, people liked me. Sharing drugs meant I had friends. At least for a little while. I was the party girl, the happy girl! I was the girl who was fun to hang with. It was a sure thing. I did it because I was afraid no one would like the real me. Not as relaxed as when I smoked. Not as wild as when I drank.

I slept around. I got obsessed with guys but never really let them see me. My role in these relationships was a "sex object." I was fun and free. I played the role I thought they wanted me to be, the role that would make them fall in love with me. I was fun and irresponsible. But it was never really right. I felt so empty and so uncomfortable with myself. I was hiding from myself.

Drugs and Alcohol Questionnaire

1. What situations, if any, do you find yourself in that encourage you to do drugs or drink?

_____

_____

_____

2. Are there certain kids who are considered "cool" because they do drugs and/or drink? Do you feel immature or "uncool" if you don't?

_____

_____

_____

3. What insecurities do you have when you are with people who do drugs or drink? How does getting high affect these insecurities?

_____

_____

_____

4. What do you think about yourself when/if you are doing drugs or drinking?

_____

_____

_____

5. Do you use drugs and alcohol to make bad feelings and thoughts go away?

_____

_____

_____

6. Write a journal entry about an actual drug/alcohol experience. If you used them, did things work out the way you wanted them to? If someone else used them, do you think things went the way they planned?

_____

_____

_____

_____

_____

_____

Self-MUTiLaTiON

Stephanie's Story

hen I was thirteen my grandfather had a stroke. My mom left to take care of him for a few weeks. I was alone with my stepfather. I was taking a shower and all of a sudden he walked in and just stood there. I said, "I'm taking a shower!" And he said he just thought I'd need a towel. Then that was it and I thought maybe I made too much of it. But then I was sleeping one night and he came in and I woke up. He started masturbating in front of me. I pretended I was asleep but I almost threw up when he leaned down and kissed me. I called my mother the next morning and begged to sleep over at Shannon's house, but she said not on a school night. Every night I lay there terrified he would come in. And then he came back and got into bed with me and molested me. He was drunk, I could tell. I ran out and grabbed the phone and called my mother. I told her what happened and she told me I must have been dreaming. She said I always have had crazy dreams and to go back to bed. I didn't know what to do. I told her I wasn't making it up and she said she had enough to deal with with Grandpa without me making up crazy stories to get her to come home. I slept on the couch with the phone, but I knew any minute he might come back. When my mom came back they were all lovey dovey and she acted like I'd never said anything. I asked her if we could have a girl talk and she looked at me like I wasn't her daughter and said she was tired, maybe another time.

I gained a lot of weight after that. I stuffed my face all the time, especially at dinner when my stepfather was there, to gross him out. I now know I was trying to make myself as unappealing as possible.

School went downhill fast. I couldn't concentrate. My grades sucked. I sat in class and played with my pencil and eraser. I gave myself eraser burns. It didn't really hurt. I poked myself with my pencil really, really hard. I sat outside smoking at lunch. I put burning matches on the inside of my elbow and pulled my arm up to watch the flame go out on my flesh. I wore long sleeves that summer. I remember the bizarre power and control I felt I was gaining as I overcame what most people would feel as pain, but I did not. I remember being proud when I showed my new friend, Nadia, how tough I was. I had achieved this ability to control my mind as well as my body. She must have thought I was crazy, and at this point, I had definitely neared the edge of insanity.

VICTIMS

When trauma lasts over a long period of time, such as childhood sexual abuse, the victim does not know how to process what is happening. Victims often feel at fault. They feel they have done something to deserve this negative treatment. They might spend a lot of time trying to figure out how they might change to stop the abuse. They feel helpless and out of control. Part of the healing must be to understand that what they have suffered is not their fault.

A person who has been victimized needs to share the experience. They need to learn to understand their feelings of shame and guilt. Once they realize that what went wrong was not their fault, they are free to experience their feelings of anger, rage and sadness. Without this healing, they are at risk for passing on their pain in the form of abuse of themselves or others.

Stephanie hurt herself and sometimes hit and abused her younger brother. Rather than feel the shame and powerlessness she felt when she was victimized, she tried to feel powerful by victimizing someone else or hurting herself. Because no one helped Stephanie or listened to her pain so she could "talk it out," she "acted it out." This is the cycle of abuse.

The healing process includes:

- Admitting the truth of what happened.
- Talking about what happened to a trusted person or people.
- Talking about how what happened made you feel and the meaning it had for you.

- Talking about how it changed the way you see yourself or life and if it changed your behavior or not.

- Understanding what you learned from this trauma that can help you grow.

One positive thing about working through painful situations while you're young is that you learn to be realistic about life. Some people expect so much of life that they set themselves up for disappointment. People who learn that life is bound to hurt sometimes and learn to work their way through it and keep hope in their hearts and a good attitude come out winners in the end.

Heartwound Story

This is what happened: _____

_____

_____

_____

This is how it made me feel: _____

_____

_____

_____

This is how it changed what I do: _____

_____

_____

_____

This is how it changed the way I see myself: _____

_____

_____

_____

This is who I'm going to tell about it: _____

_____

_____

_____

This is what I can do about it: _____

_____

_____

_____

This is what I wish could have been different about what

happened: _____

_____

_____

_____

_____

This is what I learned from the experience: _____

_____

_____

_____

_____

_____

_____

_____

This is what I will do or never do (how I will act) with what I

have learned: _____

_____

_____

_____

_____

_____

_____

_____

Section IV:

My Life: Taking Charge

*What we must decide is perhaps how we
are valuable rather than how
valuable we are.*

—EDGAR Z. FRIEDENBERG

*If we are strong our character
will speak for itself.*

—JOHN F. KENNEDY
UNDELIVERED ADDRESS, NOV. 22, 1963

*When we do the best we can, we never know
what miracle is wrought in our own life,
or in the life of another.*

—HELEN KELLER

*When a man's willing and eager,
God joins in.*

—AESCHYLUS

He that would have the fruit must climb the tree.

—THOMAS FULLER

No one knows what he can do till he tries.

—PUBLILIUS SYRUS

Separation

Who Am I When I'm on My Own?

We all get to a point where we want to become a separate person from our parents. It's confusing. It's liberating. It's painful. It's exciting. It's scary. It's called separation and individuation. Individuation is becoming a person in our own right—self-defining. It doesn't mean that we have to be physically separate and far away. It's an emotional and psychological thing. It means that we know where we leave off and someone else begins, that we're not fused in our heads with another person. We're not carbon copies. We're ourselves.

Teenage years are when this process happens the most intensely. Some of the feelings that come up around this stage of life are fear, anger, excitement, identity confusion and happiness. The peer group becomes even more important. Relationships with friends can be everything from amazing to threatening.

Some kids and parents can stay in close and comfortable communication during this phase. Other parent-kid relationships have a lot of conflict. Parents can feel rejected if they don't understand that this is a natural and important phase. They don't understand why suddenly their kids don't want to be with them all the time, why their friends are so important and they want privacy. Some parents take their kids' wishes to be separate people personally, and they wonder what they did wrong. Nothing is wrong! This is natural. If you're going to have to stand on your own two feet, you need to get some practice. The trick for both parents and kids is to learn how to separate and still stay connected. We all need support in life from the people we love. Being our own person should not mean losing the people we love. It's just part of maturing and growing into adulthood. We never outgrow our need for deep connection and supportive relationships with family and friends.

Part of the process of self-definition involves disillusionment. We learn parents aren't the perfect people we once thought they were. We learn they are only human after all. It takes getting used to, but it's also liberating because then we only have to be human, too.

Though the path of individuation can be rocky at times, it is natural and normal. Learning to stand on our own allows us to grow up. This doesn't mean we can't ask for help or lean on people. It just means we're in charge of our own lives. When we know something of who we are, we can choose a career that suits us and go after it. We can find a life partner who feels right to us. And we'll be able to find the strength, energy and excitement to go after our own lives. Standing on your own doesn't mean standing alone. We all need relationships, they're the most important part of life. We all need family in one form or another. Standing on your own means you learn to listen to your own inner guides, to fall back on your own resources and find strength within yourself. Life is an adventure, and it takes courage to really live it well.

INDIVIDUATION

To me, individuation means _____

_____

_____

What scares me about it is _____

_____

_____

_____

The thought of going off to college or having my own apartment seems _____

_____

_____

_____

I'm afraid if I'm independent I will _____

_____

_____

_____

What I'm most scared of letting go of is _____

_____

_____

_____

I never want to let go of _____

_____

_____

The scary part about being far away from my family is _____

_____

_____

_____

I will miss _____

_____

_____

I definitely will not miss _____

_____

_____

_____

What makes me most nervous about going to college or

being on my own is _____

_____

_____

_____

I'm afraid I might _____

_____

_____

Change is _____

_____

_____

The thought of leaving home makes me _____

_____

_____

I plan on always being close to my family in these ways ____

_____

_____

_____

I'll stay connected by _____

_____

_____

_____

A memory that will always be close to my heart is _____

_____

_____

_____

_____

The part of my family I carry with me in my heart is _____

_____

_____

_____

The strengths I have gained that I have inside of me are

_____

_____

_____

_____

LOOK BACK
tO LOOK FOrwarD

Sometimes you get overwhelmed with all the changes in your life. Take a few moments and think about what makes you truly happy or empowered. One way to do this is to think back to when you were a kid. Think about something you used to love to do, a hobby or activity that made you truly happy. Write a journal entry about a moment when you felt on top of the world or content and happy inside. Read Amy's story on the following pages to get some ideas.

Use the Process Pages at the back of the book for more space.

_____

_____

_____

_____

_____

_____

_____

_____

Amy's Story

I t's a beautiful day. The air is so fresh in my nose that it hurts. I can smell the pine trees and the grass heating up in the sun. I can smell the dew evaporating off the leaves and blades of grass. It smells so fresh! I can smell the water in the lake beyond the trees. I can smell the mud. I can hear birds singing.

I am fifteen and I am riding a pony. She is too small for me really, but she needed some exercise and I am the only one who wanted to help my friend out. I have two horses of my own. My big Appaloosa, Apollo, is at home, no doubt enjoying the sun also. And Dixie, my Quarter Horse/Arabian mare, is at the stable. This pony is a friend's. She hasn't ridden Queenie in a while, and Queenie is starting to get too fat. She is tan with black legs and face. In the middle of her forehead is a star. She smells very strong. I don't mind. I love the smell of horses. She needs a bath, though. And a good grooming. I decide I will do that after our ride. I am riding her bareback. My legs are warm around her fat little sides as we trot along. She is already breathing heavily. I pull her in and let her walk slowly down the trail.

The park has huge meadows that everyone rides their horses through. It is a great place to be on a sunny spring day. Riding Queenie reminds me of my first pony, Star. He was such a brat. He sure taught me how to ride. He used to bite my toes and buck me off and run home, and all sorts of things. I loved him so much. Today I miss him. Queenie, the fat little thing, reminds me of him. Queenie doesn't stand a chance against her owner's boyfriends. Poor thing. I pat her neck. She perks up a bit and starts to walk a bit faster. I wonder what she's thinking. I wonder if she misses the days we used to run on these trails together.

I start to sing under my breath, and Queenie's ears flick back at me. She slows down, listening. I start to sing songs from the musical *Oliver!* I love that musical. I start to really belt them out, really loud, singing at the top of my lungs "Food, Glorious Food!" and Queenie starts to flick her ears back and forth, and she starts to trot and I'm singing and she's trotting down the trail, past the lake, past the empty changing rooms, past the public bathrooms, down another trail toward the fields. I am singing and the sun is so warm and I feel like a kid again. I feel like I'm on Star again and I am nine years old and I don't have to ever worry about exams and school and theater stuff and auditions. It's all lifted off my shoulders. And that's how we are when around the corner comes another riding party. I stop singing, and Queenie stops dead in her tracks. I start to laugh. I can't help it. It's as if Queenie is more embarrassed than I am. They pass us by, silently trying to hide their smiles at us. Fat little Queenie with her oversized rider, bareback, slogging down the muddy spring trails. I'm sure we look funny.

I don't sing the rest of the way home. Inside I am completely warm. I feel as if Queenie and I shared something profound. I do not sing, because it would be like trying to regain the moment before. The present is perfect enough. It is enough to ride home and enjoy the sounds of the park around us and the heat of the sun on our faces. I give Queenie a bath and a brush and a lot of hugs. I don't think I will ever forget this day.

This exercise was saddening for me. I remembered the day so clearly, and it felt like I was there again. I want to be in that place again. I love animals, especially horses, and I miss the West Coast so much it brings up the sadness of leaving my old friends again. That's what my horses were to me. They were my very best friends most of the time. I used to run down to the barn every morning and evening to take care of them and be with them. I used to spend whole weekends riding. I would come home from school and hang out in the barn. Cleaning them, feeding them, grooming them, talking to them, being with them. I still love animals, and maybe I can work with them in the future.

A Letter
Of Forgiveness

Before you move forward, take a moment to move back and resolve past issues. In the space below write a letter of forgiveness. *Do not send this letter!* Either write a letter to someone you would like to forgive you, describing what happened and why you feel you need forgiveness, and asking for it. Or write a letter to yourself that you feel you deserve to receive from another person asking for your forgiveness. Use process pages for more space.

To: _____

_____

_____

_____

_____

_____

_____

_____

From : _____

A Letter to GOD

I n the space below, write a letter to God letting God know how you thank him/her for your life, your gifts, relationships or whatever you feel grateful for.

Dear God,

_____

_____

_____

_____

_____

☆ _____

☆ _____

☆ _____

☆ _____

☆ _____

☆ _____

From : _____

GraDuaTion ScrapbOOK

Memories, moments, changes, tons of personal evolution. Make a scrapbook of your life until now—start at birth and go through graduation. Put in all of the photographs that mean something to you, that tell your story, that show your life, family, friends, adventures, etc. You might also want to include drawings, memorabilia, certificates, letters, cards, anything that feels like you—that's part of your experience. Make some collage pages with lots of pictures of friends all together, or a sports page or drama page or poems—whatever. You can either put all of your pictures in a scrapbook, or photocopy them, then go to a printing store and have them spiral-bind it. This is a wonderful way to capture memories that you want to keep. It's a great present for a parent to do for you, too.

It will help you to consolidate your experience up till now with something that you can look through hundreds of times. Somehow, that helps in integrating all of it into your life and taking it with you as you move along and grow. Lots of feelings come up when you do this and that's good—you can sort of hold yourself and your experience in your own hands and look at it. When you look back at your scrapbook you'll see how far you've come, how much life you have lived. You'll notice themes. You'll see how certain parts of you have always just been there since you were small and other parts of you have really changed and grown. It's great just to look back on your own life, take hold of it and know that it is yours—in your hands to do what you want to do with it. You can take this with you and look at it whenever you like. You've done a lot of living, learning and loving. Congratulations—it's an accomplishment!

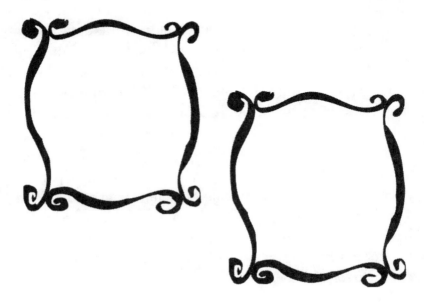

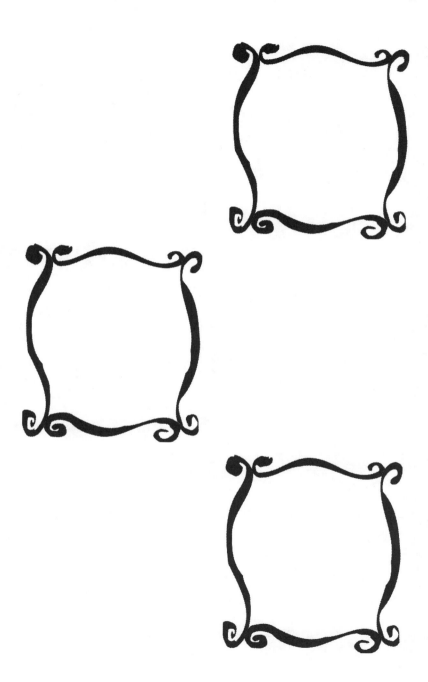

Section V:

*Character cannot be developed in
ease and quiet. Only through experience of trial
and suffering can the soul be strengthened,
vision cleared, ambition inspired
and success achieved.*

—HELEN KELLER

*Each new season grows from the
leftovers of the past. That is the essence of
change, and change is the basic law.*

—HAL BORLAND

*Through loyalty to the past,
our mind refuses to realize that tomorrow's joy is
possible only if today's makes way for it;
that each wave owes the beauty of its line only
to the withdrawal of the preceding one.*

—ANDRÉ GIDE

*Never let the future disturb you.
You will meet it, if you have to, with the same
weapons of reason, which today arm
you against the present.*

—MARCUS AURELIUS

The Word "Success"

Fill in the blanks:

When I hear the word "success," I think of _____

_____

_____

When I try to imagine a successful person I see _____

_____

_____

The part about success that makes me uncomfortable is

_____

_____

Success and my day-to-day life seem _____

_____

_____

If I let success into my life it might make me _____

_____

_____

A successful moment is a moment when _____

_____

_____

I sense success in my life when _____

_____

_____

I need more _____ to let me be okay with
success.

An activity that connects me with success and a sense of

well-being is _____

_____

I never get enough time for that because _____

_____

_____

Day-to-day success must mean _____

_____

_____

When I was young I remember _____

_____ used to make me feel so full inside.

In order to allow myself to feel good about feeling success-

ful I _____

_____

_____

_____

Attitude

Attitude is everything. A good attitude can be like the engine that drives you into a good life. Which of the following students is more likely to succeed?

"I'll never get into college," moans Jennifer. "My teachers hate me. They'll give me bad recommendations. I might as well not apply."

"I know my favorite college choice likes 'well-rounded' students, so I've been volunteering, playing intramurals and, of course, studying," says Rafael.

We can have abundance in our lives if we "go for it." We can picture what we want and let go of negative attitudes that push it away. Abundance is out there. If it's out there for other people then it's out there for you, too. The key is to first get our attitude in the right place. Then we need to release the bad attitudes that keep us feeling that we are "unlucky" or don't deserve success.

Good luck!
Your dreams can become a reality!

MAke Friends with the Fear

Creative visualization is useful in situations that are uncomfortable or that intimidate and frighten us, situations that keep us from doing things we'd like to do. If we can play these fears out in our minds by visualizing ourselves comfortable in a situation that we dread, we can reduce the fear.

If even thinking about it makes you anxious, don't force it! Breathe deeply. Think about it only to the point of anxiety. There is no rush. Picture it repeatedly until you feel comfortable. When the fear comes up, simply "witness" with the part of your mind that watches the rest of what goes on inside of you. Don't try to control it, just let it be, give it space, let it move through you and let it go. Sometimes it's our trying to control our fears or anxious thoughts that gives them more power and energy. Try just letting them be, letting them flow in and out of you without getting all involved with them. Just breathe and witness.

Little by little, let the full situation and your comfortable participation in it come into as full a view as possible. It's mental training for life.

My Mission Statement

A mission statement is a statement of intent that tells the world what something is about. Every major company out there has a mission statement announcing itself to the world. It says what it is and what it plans to do in the world. What's yours?

Mission Statement

I am: _____

_____

This is what I value: _____

_____

This is what I plan to do: _____

_____

This is how I plan to do it: _____

_____

I want my life to be: _____

_____

Personal Gifts and Strengths

We all have qualities we feel good about. We sometimes focus on the negative and forget the positive qualities we have. Write some of those qualities that have brought you this far in life. These qualities will be your strength for growth and change in building your future.

Something about myself that I am proud of _____

_____

_____

_____

_____

Some of my favorite qualities about myself _____

_____

_____

_____

_____

Some gifts that I was born with _____

_____

_____

_____

_____

_____

Some good qualities I had to work hard to develop _____

_____

_____

_____

_____

_____

The next thing I want to develop in myself _____

_____

_____

_____

_____

_____

Picturing the Life You want

Creative Visualization

*Visualization is the way we think.
Before words, images were. . . . The human
brain programs and self-programs through its image.
Riding a bicycle, driving a car, learning to read, baking a
cake, playing golf—all skills are acquired through the
image-making process. Visualization is the
ultimate consciousness tool.*

—MIKE SAMUELS, M.D., AND NANCY SAMUELS
SEEING WITH THE MIND'S EYE

Creative visualization is picturing in our minds what we would like to experience in our lives. Whether it is good friends or success in athletics or school, seeing it first in our imagination allows us to rehearse the experience over and over, and to prepare our minds to recognize aspects of the experience when they occur in our lives. We can change our "brain set," or what our brain is programmed to look for. Brain set is the way we look at life. If we believe we are lucky, we will perceive as good luck what others might see as chance. That will add to our positive self-images and cause us to be the kind of people who actively recognize and make the necessary moves and accommodations to build on that good fortune. A negative brain set can do just the opposite. But the set of our mind can be in our control.

By visualizing ourselves in situations we wish to have happen, we open the door to allow those experiences to come through.

See It, Do It

Creative Visualization

We are always making pictures in our minds. By being aware of what thoughts are in our minds and consciously visualizing our lives as we would like them to be, we use that picturing power for good rather than wasting it or, worse yet, creating self-defeating pictures.

Creative visualization is easy and pleasant to do. It can be done during quiet moments, or for a couple of seconds whenever you think of it.

1. Focus on the situation you want.
2. Picture it as if it were actually happening.
3. Use all of your senses to imagine it really happening. Touch it, talk to it, listen to it talk to you, give it color and movement.
4. Imagine it in your mind over and over again until you feel yourself in the situation, participating in it as if it were a reality. Picture it during quiet moments each day or as it occurs to you throughout the day.

I want to be awesome in the play!

I want to do well on the test!

I want to feel at home and surrounded by friends at the party.

I want to be quietly self-confident.

I want to sound **CONFIDENT** when I talk to Scott.

I'd like to play well in front of my girlfriend!

I Can Do Anything

Lauren's Monologue

I can do anything. I have the capacity to change lives. I have been through hell and back. Here I am, complete and whole. Nothing can stop me. I feel as if every part of me is alive and free. I am comfortable with my face, with my arms, with my legs, with myself. I emit positive, warm energy that just has to capture people's attention. I have a light that is coming from my soul, and it warms me and warms those around me. As I write, tears fall down my face and they are warm. I am alive and I can feel.

I take a breath in and I realize how much I have to live for. How far I have come and how much further I can go. Life is an exciting adventure, and my ride has been incredible. I am a beautiful, warm, caring, deserving person who is going to start taking care of herself. I am going to stop beating myself up and start allowing myself to fail. I am going to be as caring and tolerant of myself as I am of other people. I am going to give myself the credit I deserve and celebrate my uniqueness.

I have the strength and power to make the world just a little better. I am special, and I want to be a friend to those who are hurting. I want to wrap my arms around them and support them. I want them to feel as I feel now. I have the strength to fight and hold on. I cannot be beat. I will stand strong. There is no way around me. I am a force to be reckoned with. They must see me, really see me!

You can keep turning away from me, but I will stand here and wait. I will kiss your tears and hold you tight. I won't let you stand alone. I will hold your hand every step of the way. I will be your friend. I have the strength for two. Lean on me until you find your way. When you want to walk away, I will celebrate and honor your strength and let you go with open arms. I will love you. There is nothing you can do to change or alter this love.

I am lucky to be me. I am lucky to have the ability to notice the world. To feel the world. To believe people care about each other. Sometimes words get in the way. I can help people get past those words and find their feelings.

Life, come at me full force. I can handle anything. I relish the opportunity to experience. I want to feel love . . . I want to feel pain . . . every experience is essential to my journey, the journey to becoming the best person I can be. I want to live every moment to the fullest. To love beyond reason. I don't want to worry about the consequences. I just want to feel. I will survive.

Thank you, God . . . thank you for my sensitivity, thank you for my heart, thank you for my soul, thank you for my body, thank you for my life. Please let me return some of what I have been given. Please allow me the strength to move on and continue to grow.

EmOTiOnal
MAd (SAd, GladD Lib

I can be very strong and determined when I want to be.

The activities I do now that I think help to build strength in

me are _____ and _____.

(activity)   (activity)

The special abilities I develop from them are _____

(abilities)

and _____. In my future I would like to be

(abilities)

_____. I have goals for myself. They are

(adjective or noun)

_____ and

(phrase)

_____.

(phrase)

If they don't work out, I can _____.

(phrase)

I have liked to _____ since I was little. When I

(verb)

think of taking charge of my day, I _____.

_____.

(phrase)

My concern about taking charge is _____

_____.
(phrase)

The activities that make me feel strong and active are

_____, _____
(noun)   (noun or verb)

and _____. I feel _____
(noun or verb)   (adjective)

when I think about my future. I know I can succeed most of

the time if I really put my mind to it. I feel successful when I

_____ and
(phrase)

_____.
(phrase)

Have a Plan

Jim Carrey was once a broke, out of work, stand-up comic. He dated a check to himself ten years in the future for ten million dollars. Ten years later, on that day, he received ten million dollars for a movie.

Write down on paper what your plan for yourself is. Write down where you want to be in your life and visualize it as if it were already true. See it, smell it, taste it and feel it!

MISSION
STATEMENT

I am: _____

_____

_____

How I would change the world: _____

_____

_____

How I can be part of that change: _____

_____

_____

I want my life to be: _____

_____

_____

Process Pages

We're not always clear on what's going through our minds—especially if something is confusing or feels big. When we journal on Process Pages, our thoughts and feelings sort of unravel themselves on the paper. Pretty soon, whatever's on our minds finds its way to words and sentences.

We don't need to know what we want to say before we write it. In fact, it's almost better if we don't.

Let your mind grow onto the Process Pages however it wants to. The idea is not to say it right or perfectly. Just get what's on your mind or heart out onto the paper. You might be amazed at how much clarity comes just through letting this process happen.

There's nothing more empowering than getting to know who we are on the inside—PUTTING WORDS TO FEELINGS AND FEELINGS TO WORDS™. This is how we become emotionally literate—able to READ our emotions.

The page is yours—do with it what you like. ENJOY. Let your inner depths emerge.